HealthTech
GIANT
SLAYER

Praise For
Health Tech Giant Slayer

"*Health Tech Giant Slayer* delivers the ultimate field guide for underdog CEOs and revenue leaders who are ready to fight smarter, not harder. Fred Sheffield distills decades of front-line revenue growth experience into a powerful system that turns scrappy startups into strategic powerhouses. With the clarity of a battlefield strategist and the heart of a coach, Fred shows us how to ditch the generic playbook and build a buyer's journey that wins respect, unlocks revenue, and earns a seat at the table. If you're a founder or growth leader in health tech, this book isn't just a read—it's a reckoning."

Colt Briner, Author of *The Race to Relevance* and Founder of Scrappy AF Solutions

"Fred's book, *Health Tech Giant Slayer*, is compelling, methodically built, full of insights, a true playbook in GTM and scale efforts, and conveys how to drive accountability within a performance culture. At its core, it's disruptive with respect to the traditional legacy mindset, instead laying out a deliberate plan on how to create value and growth within today's complicated market ecosystem. It's clear that Fred's eye on true business development efforts is rooted within his professional career journey."

Terry Snyder, President Helixa Advisory, and Fortune 100 and PE backed Healthcare Executive

"Although Fred and I worked together for a short time, the impact was immediate. Many of the go-to-market systems discussed in his book energized the culture, strengthened our pipeline, and brought predictability to our forecast within a few short months. I highly recommend *Health Tech Giant Slayer* to any CEO looking for a practical, measurable system to scale their GTM team with confidence."

Vik Krishnan, CEO of Instem,
former CEO & President of TeleVox Healthcare

Health Tech
GIANT
SLAYER

What CEOs Need To Know To Defeat Their Goliaths

Fred L. Sheffield

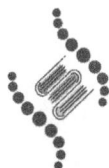

**HEALTH
AUTHORITY
BOOKS**

HealthTech GIANT SLAYER
What CEOs Need To Know To Defeat Their Goliaths

ISBN-13: 978-1-966168-28-7
Library of Congress Control Number: 2025910893

Designed by Melissa Farr, Back Porch Creative LLC

HEALTH AUTHORITY BOOKS
2511 WOODLANDS WAY
OCEANSIDE, CA 92054
www.indiebooksintl.com

Health Authority Books® is an imprint of Indie Books International, Inc.

Contents

Preface

This book is a David-versus-Goliath story. Throughout my career, I have worked with David-type CEOs of health tech companies, from startups to scaleups.

These health tech Davids want predictable and sustainable growth. To do so, they need to slay the Goliaths of their industry.

I assume many of you reading this book want to accomplish the same for your organizations. You have concluded that in order to level up, you need to compete differently. With over twenty-five years in health tech sales, I have learned that trying to compete like a Goliath when you are a David is not the answer. You must accept who you are and come to the market with greater intention, discipline, and a rock-solid plan for all aspects of your go-to-market execution.

I see so many organizations going to battle following the wrong strategy, leveraging the wrong processes, and with the wrong people, which leads to random and inconsistent execution and, worse yet, inconsistent revenue. As a result, their lack of internal predictability makes them very predictable externally, which is the complete opposite of what made David such a dangerous warrior.

I know what it feels like to be a David, an underdog. Quite frankly, I know what it feels like to be underestimated as an underdog. I have been CRO (Chief Revenue Officer) at four different David-sized companies, probably similar to yours. And through trial and error, fighting the battles like David, I learned to do things differently and win. I learned how to channel being underestimated to fuel my passion for creating systems to drive high double-digit growth. I want you to win. I want you to defeat your Goliaths. That's my purpose for writing this book. I intend to help you compete differently and more effectively so you can scale quickly, outperform larger competitors, and exceed your financial goals.

This book provides the five stones you need to slay your giants. It's a proven system that, when practiced, will help you succeed.

Fred L. Sheffield
Charlotte, North Carolina

PART I

Size Doesn't Matter, But Execution Does

1

Why Health Tech Underdogs Can Win

A re you a health tech company suffering from inconsistent growth that feels like you are fighting giants? Your struggle may be a David and Goliath story.

Regardless of one's faith, most people in the Western world recognize the classic story of David and Goliath. This is the story of a mere shepherd boy with just a sling who battled an armored giant. This is how the first book of Samuel tells the story:

> *Now when the words which David spoke were heard, they reported them to Saul; and he sent for him.*
>
> *Then David said to Saul, "Let no man's heart fail because of him; your servant will go and fight with this Philistine."*

And Saul said to David, "You are not able to go against this Philistine to fight with him; for you are a youth, and he a man of war from his youth."

But David said to Saul, "Your servant used to keep his father's sheep, and when a lion or a bear came and took a lamb out of the flock,

I went out after it and struck it, and delivered the lamb from its mouth; and when it arose against me, I caught it by its beard, and struck and killed it.

Your servant has killed both lion and bear; and this uncircumcised Philistine will be like one of them, seeing he has defied the armies of the living God."

…And Saul said to David, "Go, and the Lord be with you!"

So Saul clothed David with his armor, and he put a bronze helmet on his head; he also clothed him with a coat of mail.

David fastened his sword to his armor and tried to walk, for he had not tested them. And David said to Saul, "I cannot walk with these, for I have not tested them." So David took them off.

Then he took his staff in his hand; and he chose for himself five smooth stones from the brook, put them in the pouch of his shepherd's bag, in a pouch which he had, and his sling was in his hand. And he drew near to the Philistine.

Then David put his hand in his bag and took out a stone; and he slung it and struck the Philistine in his forehead, so that the stone sank into his forehead, and he fell on his face to the earth.

So David prevailed over the Philistine with a sling and a stone, and struck the Philistine and killed him. But there was no sword in the hand of David.

Therefore David ran and stood over the Philistine, took his sword and drew it out of its sheath and killed him, and cut off his head with it.

1 Sam. 17:31—40, 17:49–51 (New King James Version)[1]

David trusted his skills that had saved him and his flock from countless lions and bears. He became fearless and confident in his abilities to take down those predators to rescue his sheep. In doing so, he became practiced in his process.

In Malcolm Gladwell's 2013 book, *David and Goliath: Underdogs, Misfits, and the Art of Battling Giants*, Gladwell also talks about how Goliath probably had acromegaly, which made him bigger yet caused him to have reduced mobility and eyesight. Being a smaller individual made David nimble and adaptable to changing conditions while still leveraging his unique and unconventional skills.[2]

Let's Contemplate David And The Five Stones

There have been many theories and speculations as to why David decided to choose five stones to go to battle with the giant. The prevailing belief is that David knew that Goliath had four other brothers, so when he picked the stones from the brook, he took one for each potential opponent should he need to do battle with them all. That demonstrated incredible confidence in his ability to execute and the foresight to plan for all possible challenges presented by the situation. Even so, the odds were stacked against him.

Both an impossibility of victory and an improbability of victory are happening simultaneously. The impossibility of victory is around David and Goliath's supposed difference in skill sets. Goliath had been a trained man of war his entire life, whereas David had been a shepherd boy tending his family's sheep. Logic would tell you that there was a larger, more experienced competitor on the battlefield. The reality was that they had trained in different ways, but no less fiercely in their regard, and Goliath severely underestimated his opponent.

The improbability of victory was overcome by David's strong faith in his purpose (his why) and what made him unique. He probably had only one shot at best to kill Goliath and had to have unwavering confidence in his process such that it was instinctual.

I have heard it said that everything had to align perfectly in order for this victory to come about. This included the right stone being chosen, the sling being well maintained, the trajectory of the shot, the velocity of the stone after being launched, the angle at which the stone was launched, and Goliath's armor that could have blocked the stone from hitting and causing a mortal wound. The list goes on and on. And that does not even account for the improbability that a young shepherd boy would have the skill set and the faith to raise his hand and say, "I can slay the giant."

What is also important to note about this story is that King Saul, who was the leader of the nation of Israel in the day, also had to share David's faith in their purpose and believe in his unique ability to execute. Regardless of the brevity of the circumstance, King Saul had to be bought in, which demonstrated unwavering confidence in David's unconventional approach to invigorating the self-assuredness of his army. Both were necessary for David to win against a much larger and supposedly superior rival.

As with a smaller organization, the preparation that David did is what trumped the improbability factor. *Size does not matter when unrelenting preparation drives execution.* That preparation must align with your unique situation and skill set, or you might as well pack up and go home. If your preparation is one-size-fits-all, you have no chance of winning.

Going Up Against Your Goliath

You should be asking yourself:

- "What makes me different?

- What makes my approach to solving client problems truly unique?

- What's the process I need to execute to take down a larger opponent?

- How can I become internally predictable with how I execute so that I can be unpredictable when facing my competitors?"

All those questions will help you practice and be ready to win.

CB Insights conducted 111 post-mortems and published a study on the top reasons startups fail. The top reasons are as follows: 38 percent ran out of cash and were unable to raise new capital. Burning through cash without well-designed strategy and processes is simply guessing and a recipe for disaster. For 35 percent, the study found no market need for the product or service. This clearly shows a poor understanding of the Total Addressable Market (TAM) vs. the Serviceable Addressable Market (SAM) for the company's solution (we'll discuss this in more detail in a later chapter).

Another 20 percent were outcompeted. For me, this is the saddest statistic of all. It is a clear indicator of a lack of understanding of themselves, market awareness, competition, and a repeatable strategy to compete differently.

Another 19 percent had a flawed business model, which is an example of lacking predictable internal processes. Price and cost issues and not having the right team were 15 percent and 14 percent, respectively.[3] This is another example of a lack of understanding of the SAM and the right hiring profiles to win in those markets.

What if David wore the armor that everyone else was telling him to wear, having never worn it before, and tried to use his sling? Would he have had enough time to make the necessary changes in his strategy to win, or would Goliath have simply run him down? Are you fighting your battles wearing a strategy that doesn't fit your unique skill set or size? Are you becoming encumbered by processes that are one-size-fits-all, which is affecting your ability to take advantage of being nimble and unpredictable?

Instead of worrying about what the larger or more established health tech company is doing, embrace your unique skill set and flip the script as David did. Being an underdog can be challenging, but with the right processes in place, it can also be fun and turn your organization into a predictable winner.

Why The Health Tech Industry Needs This Book

Health tech has a diverse client segmentation, from individual-provider practices to large, multi-facility health systems with a laundry list of specialties and subspecialties. This range of diversity can have a big impact on how decisions are made. In addition, there is the complexity of the mix of for-profit, nonprofit, and government facilities, which each operate with different processes and agendas.

Throughout the range of differences, one key factor prevails. These organizations exist with the mission to serve and treat patients and their families with sensitivity and compassion as a top priority rather than with a pure profit motive, as with many other businesses. As a result, this requires a very different approach and, quite frankly, a very different hiring profile for your go-to-market team.

The TAM itself presents challenges, with 407 health systems controlling 67 percent of US hospitals and 76 percent of all hospital beds.[4] The consolidation extends to physician practices, where 80 percent of physicians are employed by hospitals or corporate entities.[5] With the limited TAM and mission-driven decision process, traditional selling does not work, nor should it.

This complexity of decisions becomes even more challenging with the interconnected web of stakeholders and decision points. Convincing the business side of a department or facility isn't enough. The ability to navigate and build consensus with the complexities of different functions within an organization is often the difference between winning and losing. From the finance team and the challenges of reimbursements to fund the mission to the diversity required of the IT teams that support the organization, all present unique obstacles compared to other businesses.

For health tech startups and scaleups, these market dynamics create significant barriers to entry. Traditional sales approaches focusing solely on product demonstrations, pricing discussions, and unsophisticated closing techniques have proven inadequate and unacceptable in this sophisticated environment. Additionally, established competitors often have deep-rooted relationships and proven track records, making it difficult for new entrants to gain traction without a more nuanced approach.

The purpose of this book is to guide health tech startups and scaleup organizations by the following:

- Creating a differentiated buying experience that delivers more value than your well-established competitors

- Developing strategies to find and engage with qualified opportunities

- Leveraging the purchase experience and qualified opportunities to run repeatable, scalable systems to make revenue generation more predictable

- Forming a go-to-market team culture with the right people and mindset to slay your Goliaths

Winning in health tech is not easy, and this book serves as a strategic resource to help your organization navigate the intricate landscape of healthcare sales. It all starts with a strategy of doing things differently, as it did with David as he stepped onto the battlefield against the giant.

My Goliath Story Did Not Go According To Plan

This is the story of my ground zero when I realized I had to do things differently. I come from a family of underdogs like David. My father lacked a strong education background, yet he overachieved by creating a very successful business. This underdog mentality was always a badge of honor. However, I never considered how my dad's story might affect my journey and become the foundation for the 5 Stones Growth Systems.

I had always been a pretty decent salesperson, but I did it the way other folks do. I relied primarily on relationships. I was a likable Southern guy, which would grant me access to people. In fact, I could gain access to key executives without a ton of effort.

One particular executive ran a two-thousand-bed health system. He and I had established a good rapport, and based on that rapport, he brought me in to run the process on a very high-profile software decision.

When we got into the process, I disappointed him. I had difficulty going beyond likability to the execution of a strategy. I had the upper hand on the deal, but I allowed someone else to out-compete me because they ran a more structured process. They won the value creation game.

They were more strategic and value-oriented. They were able to align with and help shape the client's vision. Honestly, all I had going for me was that they liked me. And I lost the deal. The executive who really cared for me sat me down and told me why I lost.

He told me, "It is definitely important for people to like you. It is equally important for people to respect you. When you learn to do that, you will be deadly." That was devastating to hear.

Because of my upbringing and watching my dad win against improbable odds, I sucked it up and went to work. I became a student of sales strategy. When I joined the healthcare technology company Pyxis Corporation, I worked my way up through the organization to become one of their top sellers year after year. After Pyxis was acquired by Cardinal Health, I was often involved in helping to shape the sales strategy for the company. This experience gave me even more insight into the importance of working a repeatable process to deliver value and gain respect by the customer.

I studied the Sandler Selling System, the Miller Heiman sales process, Jeff Thull, SPIN Selling, countless books on executive presence, and eventually, *The Challenger Sale*, which became an integral part of the sales strategy at CareFusion after its spinoff from Cardinal Health. To enhance my skills, I even took a sales leadership role at SAVO, the original sales enablement platform.

I eventually landed my first Chief Revenue Officer (CRO) position in health tech. In my very first executive role, I took the skills that I had developed over the prior twelve-plus years of my career, and much like David, I created a predictable and consistent approach that over a three-year period led to 4X growth for a bootstrapped, founder-led, health tech company. Now, I've dedicated my life to working with CEOs of startups to scaleups in health tech with companies that want predictable and sustainable growth.

2

There Must Be A Repeatable Growth System

John C. Maxwell once said, "Small disciplines repeated with consistency every day lead to great achievements gained slowly over time." At the heart of the 5 Stones Growth Systems are the daily disciplines that drive the process of leading the buyer's journey with an effective and proficient strategy. However, other systems, when lacking a disciplined approach, will affect the success of your go-to-market team. A systematic approach to those as well is needed to create predictable growth for your organization.

The Ten Growth Killers That Can Hold Your Company Back

I have been doing this work for a long time, and in my decades of work, I have found ten growth killers that can take down any health tech company at any time:

1. Misaligned expectations with the executive team, investors, board, or founder

2. No clarity around why and what makes the company unique, how it singularly solves problems, and how it delivers differentiated insight to its prospects. This goes deeper than the mission, vision, and values posted on the walls and recited during team meetings.

3. A lack of clarity around the TAM versus the SAM, as well as confusion about the ICP and the key influencers or personas.

4. A lack of a documented buying process with a common shorthand language for the entire company to understand progress on all deals, which prevents everyone from being on the same page with strategy and discourages collaboration and understanding

5. A lack of alignment within the go-to-market team or random acts of go-to-marketing execution

6. A loss of accountability with objectives and key results (OKRs) or other key initiatives that are critical for growth

7. Ignoring metrics that matter—a lack of a scorecard that is reviewed weekly to determine if key performance indicators are trending in the right direction

8. The silent killer of a poor culture: underappreciating team members and not fostering psychological safety

9. The delusion of "playing it safe" and competing like everyone else

10. An inability to figure out how to defeat larger and better-funded competitors or to develop a differentiated experience for the client

The challenge with all these stems from a lack of repeatable systems that organize and track data points early on for predictability. Everyone is focused on performance—which they should be—but without standardized systems that track key elements or milestones, you will never spot early trends to pivot until you've wasted resources and time on a flawed strategy.

Even worse, without repeatable systems, random acts and constant pivots not supported by data will happen, which weakens trust with the company, leadership team, investors, and the board. Sadly, far too often, I see really talented leaders lose their jobs and great ideas die because of random acts of execution. We will get into the mechanics of how the 5 Stones Growth Systems will help overcome these growth killers in the next section, but first, I want to lay out two core principles of the system to drive success.

The Secret Sauce Is How Your Company Orchestrates The Buyer's Journey

Arguably the all-time cult movie for sales is *Glengarry Glen Ross* with Blake (actor Alec Baldwin's character) pushing the ABCs of selling (always be closing). This spoof on selling, based on a play from the 1980s, is entertaining but could not be more opposite from the systems discussed in this book. The misaligned strategy for Blake's company Premier Properties starts with "the leads" from Mitch and Murray, who lacked an understanding of their ideal customer, and then moves to the dubious sales tactics of the sales team with their jobs on the line.

The interesting thing is that I see this same type of "salesy" push today in health tech, with an account executive (AE) rushing to demo, pushing out a proposal for their product, and using all the predictable closing techniques of the early 1980s to "get the deal done!"

The AE incorrectly thinks that by conducting a little discovery and sharing the demo with a healthcare organization, the benefits of the product will just miraculously be clear. The issue with that, first and foremost, is that it's not about you, but that's the message you are sending to health system decision-makers.

As we discussed above, health systems do not function like other businesses with the primary focus on profits, but rather they focus on the mission of healthcare as the ultimate outcome. Demos and proposals are important, but gaining a deep understanding of the market and how your organization specifically fits to drive value is by far more meaningful in decision-making.

Countless studies have shown that the buying experience is the number one indicator of customer loyalty.[6] Creating a differentiated experience starts with understanding the prospect's why, which may be hidden. The health tech company that can deliver an insightful conversation and lead a prospect to think differently about how to solve real-world problems wins. I promise that you will be able to deliver more demos and proposals when you get that right. More importantly, when value creation becomes a part of the fabric of your organization, you will be viewed differently than your more established competitors and create predictable growth without being salesy like Blake.

Early Indicators Matter Deeply

I know we've all heard the hockey analogy by Wayne Gretzky: focus on where the puck is going. When it comes to designing internal predictable systems to stop the growth killers, you need to first focus on the puck. I'm not a hockey enthusiast, but I know that a lot of focus is placed on the correct form to maneuver a slap shot to make it past multiple defenders, the goalie, and into a twenty-four-square-foot goal. The calculations to perform this feat are leading indicators. They are repeatable and give the hockey player the greatest chance to consistently score against their competitor.

It's the same with baseball. Players spend hours at batting practice, honing the leading indicators that will enable them to make good contact. When they need a home run in a game situation, they are not focused on the fence but on the ball. The goal is for the leading indicators of the mechanics to become instinctual so that the outcome becomes more predictable.

And it was the same with David—he was focused on his technique to kill the giant, not solely on the giant itself. That's the difference between leading and lagging indicators and why they are so important. We all want the outcome of the lagging indicator, but we must focus on the leading indicators first.

My Personal Example

Best-selling author Jeff Thull published his book, *The Prime Solution: Close the Value Gap, Increase Margins, and Win The Complex Sale*, in 2005.[7] I was honored that one of my wins, when I was an AE with Pyxis, was discussed in his book on page 136. The win was a massive team effort that included the product team, the marketing team, the clinical team, and company leadership. With all humility, the sheer size of the initial deal and commitment was legendary with the sales organization at Pyxis for years.

As a company, we did a lot of things right during the eighteen-month decision process. Understanding and formulating a strategy of leading indicators or key milestones was critical to managing the process both internally and externally. Yes, we demoed and yes, we provided proposals, but the intricate process of executing on creating value was the difference between winning and losing.

All of the leading indicators in this opportunity started in the very beginning. The client, a prestigious health system, saw early on that we understood their real-world challenges, and that we delivered insight to get them thinking differently about how to solve their challenges. We aligned with the key influencer in this decision, who introduced us to the leadership team. We engaged the leadership team as a whole to shape their vision with our strategy.

In fact, we had their entire decision team fly to our headquarters to meet and design what the end game would look like well before the contract was signed. None of what we did happened by chance. We created predictable results with our internal strategy, which created a very different and uncommon experience for the health system and a unique buying experience for the client.

Additionally, I corrected a lot of my mistakes from my "ground zero" loss mentioned earlier. I unlocked the incredible value of being liked and respected in a major way. Your AEs can as well when your organization starts leading and coaching with the principles outlined in this book.

As a former general manager, I have walked in your shoes. I have discovered that the more you can create systems within your organization, the more unpredictable you can be when facing larger, more well-funded competitors, and the more proactive you can be with key measurements that ensure predictable outcomes and optimize shareholder value.

PART II

The 5 Stones Growth Systems

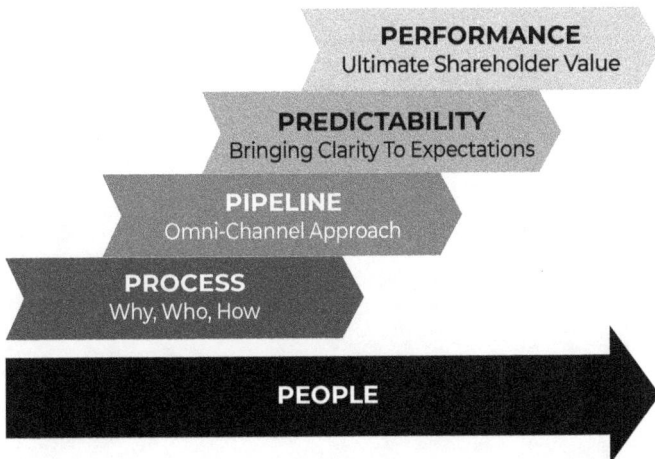

PERFORMANCE
Ultimate Shareholder Value

PREDICTABILITY
Bringing Clarity To Expectations

PIPELINE
Omni-Channel Approach

PROCESS
Why, Who, How

PEOPLE

n the David and Goliath story, not only is there the daily preparation of mastering the slingshot, but there is also the requirement of picking the right stone.

It's no different with the systems I will introduce to you in this book. The five stones or systems that comprise the 5 Stones Growth Systems are *process, pipeline, predictability, performance*, and brought to life by your *people*. The order in which you execute the system is critical as well. Boards are crystal clear on the performance numbers that are expected on a monthly, quarterly, and annual basis. Still, when it comes to execution, the water starts getting murky—especially in the startup and scaleup environment.

The endgame of performance is important. As former NFL coach Bill Parcells famously said, "You are what your record says you are." But I have witnessed countless annual planning exercises where it's all about coming to an agreement using spreadsheets on a revenue number to back into a budget, hoping that the organization can find a way to be predictable and that they have enough pipeline to get them there.

The interesting part is that systems created to drive the go-to-market process often lack true strategy and/or are random in nature. When the numbers are presented to the people, they question, complain, or check out because they don't have a clear understanding of the game plan or a systemic strategy to get them there. Even worse, the answer can often be to throw more people at a broken process. Randomness becomes a snowball rolling downhill, and predictability is a distant dream.

Sequence Matters

To ignite growth and create a repeatable, coachable, and measurable go-to-market strategy, the sequence in which you design your systems matter. You may feel you are already targeting many of the stones in the 5 Stones Growth Systems today. But do you have a framework built around each so that you can pinpoint what's working well and what needs improvement? Are you being intentional and leveraging each function to build on the other, creating momentum as opposed to being reactive when performance is flat or declining?

Whether designed or by happenstance, you have a system. When it is random by nature, I see the following sequence. The expectations for how sales are performing come under question. Pressure is put on the team to become more predictable and to add more pipeline because the current pipeline opportunities are weak. They have a "sales process," but no one really adheres to it because no one truly sees value in it. Anxiety gets hyped up, and the salespeople stress and double down on their own ideas of how to sell more stuff. This creates skepticism in the company's leadership and fosters a broken culture.

The broken sequence looks like this:

> **Performance > Predictability > Pipeline > Process**
>
> **People**

The reality is that the system should be designed and managed the complete opposite way, starting with process. In the 5 Stone Growth Systems, process involves three components: *why, who,* and *how.* Why are we in business, and why are we unique in our market? Once you truly understand your purpose and what makes you unique, you have the insight to properly diagnose your TAM (your who) to clarify the accounts you can most effectively target. When you understand what a qualified target looks like, it provides the insight required to design an effective buying process on how to executive and lead prospects to a decision.

Having clearly documented your why, who, and how, you can be much more effective at designing your pipeline strategy for laser-focused targeting, leading to a believable and qualified pipeline. The buying process you have designed should be the repeatable strategy the team follows to lead the prospect to a decision.

The combination of targeting the right prospects with your unique value through a well-designed strategy that leads to a decision for a qualified pipeline opportunity unlocks predictability and a believable system to forecast. Performance will happen with full buy-in across the organization and when followed religiously and with rigor. If not, you have a well-documented system in place that tracks all components to quickly complete a root-cause analysis and make calculated, as opposed to random, pivots. In addition, you are empowering your people by equipping them with the tools, training, and motivation to excel.

The correct sequence to design effect go-to-market growth systems is the following:

Process > Pipeline > Predictability > Performance
People

In this section of the book, we will break down each of the stones of the 5 Stones Growth Systems, taking a deep dive into tactics and strategies to leverage as building blocks to create internal predictability for accelerated growth. I will share how to create a succinct plan for each stone so that your team can focus on execution, and you and your leadership will have a reliable system to measure performance.

Each system provides flexibility for you to encourage creativity and room to add your specific market nuances. Think of the systems as frameworks or a set of guardrails to drive the success of your company's sales and marketing activities.

The end game will be a collective strategy that enables your organization to compete differently and more effectively than your larger Goliaths.

The first step is to look at your process.

3

Stone One:
Process

Everyone may be interested in success, but few truly value the process behind it.

Process is not just about being repeatable. It is also about being predictable internally in your approach so you can quickly determine what is accelerating opportunities and any steps that need correcting. If you approach something differently every time, there is no opportunity for improvement because nothing is measurable.

The concept of process is extremely important. As mentioned above, it's the foundation for all the five stones. It's creating a system that is actually the star, regardless of talent. And when executed properly, it will quickly provide clarity around your team and their ability to execute. It can make your A players much stronger, and it can evaluate quickly whether B and C players can become A players.

We see it all the time in the NFL with really strong organizations that are able to bring in role players to fit the system and see superstars become even better. Take Brock Purdy as an example. He was "Mr. Irrelevant" in the 2022 NFL draft, meaning he was the last person drafted that year. For those who do not follow football, 261 players were selected ahead of him, and his position—quarterback—is considered to be the most important position on the field of play. Those drafted last rarely make the team, much less become the starting quarterback for an NFL contender, but that's exactly what he did. His coach, Kyle Shannan, said, "The system should be the star." Brock Purdy is proof of that concept.

A lot of organizations focus on tactics. Tactics without a strategy are worthless. They are not repeatable, not measurable, and will not affect your organization's long-term growth. You've got to put a system into place that works and levels up your team to achieve maximum production.

We will cover three main components in this chapter: why, who, and how. Process starts with understanding why your organization is unique. Once you clearly understand what separates you from the market, then you need to determine who (ideal customers) you can and should focus on within your market for maximum results. Finally, you build out how you execute with documented critical milestones that act as leading indicators that you are leading a repeatable, predictable buying experience with your prospect.

Getting Clarity On Your Internal Why And What Makes You Unique

To develop strong growth systems, everyone in the organization must be clear about why and what makes them unique. It's amazing how many organizations I work with that do not have a clear understanding of this. As a result, their differentiators are shallow or nonexistent.

One of the first questions I always ask a CEO (often putting them on the spot) is, "Why are you in business, and what are the three things that make you different from your competitors?" You would be surprised how many can't answer that question or fumble with their words rambling on to provide something. If the CEO can't succinctly answer it, how do you expect the rest of the company to be aligned?

When I moved into the general manager role at one of my previous companies, one of the first actions I took was to bring the leadership team together to define our why and the three things that made us unique in the market. Once defined, it became a part of every prospect discussion and also a gauge for product development.

Here is what we came up with. We were a patient payment platform, and our why was to "make healthcare accessible for everybody." Sounds simple, but there is a lot behind that statement. First, we all know about high-deductible health insurance plans. Back when we all had low deductibles, we were just concerned about getting better. Now, with high-deductible plans, first we worry about whether we can afford the care, and then we worry if we will get better. Our platform helped eliminate the first concern about affordability, which leads to accessibility so that patients could focus on the second part: getting better.

What made us unique was that we (1) created peace of mind for patients, (2) brought cash in the door faster for providers, and (3) reduced payment complexity. Simple words, but once again a lot behind those phases led to the way our specific solution was designed.

To put this into context, our largest client was close to churning. As the general manager, I went to the health system to meet with the leadership team as we were sunsetting our legacy platform and looking to move them to our newly designed SaaS solution. The health system took this opportunity to shop the market to see what else might be available before making a final decision.

I opened the meeting with a slide that simply showed our why and the three points that made us unique. This opened the discussion and it was clear that we aligned with what they felt was important to their business as well. I then led them through how the SaaS solution addressed each of these points better than our legacy solution and our competitors.

It created an engaging discussion with the leadership team, and we maintained their business.

As a CEO, you not only need succinct clarity around your why and your uniques for your go-to-market team, but also as the north star for your organization.

Uncovering The Who Or The Total Addressable Market

The next step to building repeatable systems is to very clearly understand your who, your total addressable market (TAM), and how much of the TAM your product can actually service. Who truly is your ideal customer? What does that ideal customer profile (ICP) look like, and what personas within that organization do you want to target? Essentially, you are bringing product/market fit to life for all your go-to-market activities.

I love the television show *Shark Tank* and you see this mistake in a microcosm happen all the time. Hypothetically, a budding entrepreneur making a pitch to the "sharks" (potential funders) might make a statement that the global soft drink market is $450 billion and the projected growth rate is 5 percent over the next x number of years. "If we capture one percent of that market, we'll all be rich!"

The sharks then proceed to rip them apart as maybe the pitch being made is for a probiotic soft drink for gut health, and they know that someone who is pounding high-sugar and highly caffeinated soft drinks could care less about gut health. This is the difference between the TAM and the market you can serve—and understanding the difference and everything about it.

In health tech, I've seen this mistake set companies back by months and years, blow up annual budgets, and miss revenue. For example, I was speaking with a CRO recently who shared that the organization she recently joined had a huge miss in identifying their SAM and ICP, which set them back by six months.

If you have existing customers and have been in business long enough to have existing data, you can start by looking at the historical data of opportunities in your customer relationship management database (CRM) that you've won in the past. However, most startups and scaleups don't always have this data and must start from scratch.

The first step is to build out what a qualified and unqualified ICP looks like. Once identified, build these data points into your CRM for tracking. Some companies can sell you pretty extensive data on health systems, hospitals, and providers to assist with the qualification process, or you can do it manually. The manual process is labor intensive, but if that's what it takes to get it done, do it. It's that important because it can have a dramatic impact on strategy, budgets, and revenue.

Determining How You Build Your Buying Process

Once you know why you are unique and who you should target, the next step focuses on how you execute. Many sales organizations refer to this as the sales process. Companies spend tons of money on this process, but in many cases, it never gets used because it is not considered a strategy for success or a living, breathing operating system.

This is the methodology of how your sales team goes to market. I prefer to refer to it as a buying process. It is at the heart of creating the buying experience. The buying process includes the key milestones that, when executed correctly and in the right sequence, can tell you how you are performing and how the opportunity is advancing. These are the leading indicators for success. Getting this right is critical for creating predictability with your forecasting model.

To make it actionable, fields must be created within your CRM to document the strategy sequentially so that it can create a shorthand language to tell the story of the opportunity for consistency and to be measurable for predictability.

Designing the buying process is one of the most important steps in the 5 Stones Growth Systems. Regardless of solution or market segment, there are a few critical milestones that I have found important for qualifying an opportunity and leading a prospect to a decision.

Finding Your Key Influencer And Accessing The Decision Group

Everyone knows that you've got to find your champion within an organization. I want you to be thinking more strategically. It isn't just about someone who will take your call, share details about the organization, and generally "likes you." It's someone who will actively evangelize on your behalf when you win their respect and get them thinking differently about their business. This person also needs to be someone who has the power to influence other key decision-makers because, in enterprise healthcare, decisions are almost always made by groups of people. Think of this person as a strategic ally, not as someone who will do your work for you. You still need to lead the process.

This is not to say you shouldn't target other personas within the potential buying committee. In fact, I have a time-tested process that I implement with my teams for mapping out all of the key decision-makers on an opportunity. (Go to www.5Stonesgrowth.com/tools to download a free copy.) But at the very top of the reasons for losing a deal or ending in no decision is that we didn't identify and engage *the* key influencer.

Influencers in general, whether positive or negative (classic blockers), fall into three categories: product, process, and performance. Product influencers are the ones who push for

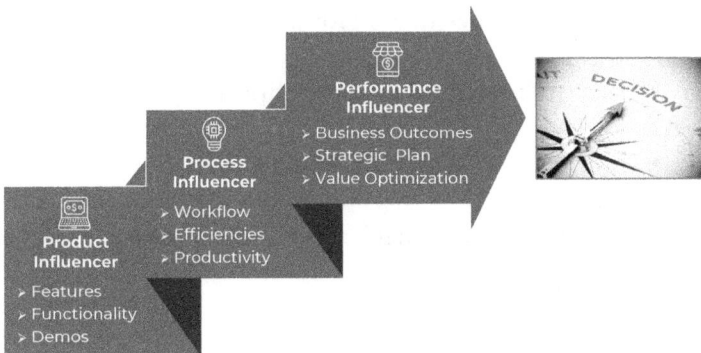

Figure 1

the demo. They want to see how the product works, focusing on features and benefits to compare to their existing solution.

Next are process influencers, who are looking at how the solution will improve staff productivity. They are focused on workflow and improving efficiencies.

Finally, there are the performance influencers. These influencers are more strategic and listen to see how your solution will affect organizational outcomes. How will your offering align with the health system's strategic plan?

All influencers are important and, to some degree, have characteristics of each of the three categories in their makeup in some way. But I have found that performance-dominant influencers are the ones who are thinking much bigger and can drive change and affect risk aversion. Performance influencers are almost always the key influencer who can act as an ally or strategic partner when orchestrating a buying decision.

There are qualities to look for in your key influencer:

- They are not afraid to take political risks.

- They command organizational respect.

- They understand that organizational advancement is critical to their success.

- They are open to new concepts.

- Regardless of their title, they are sought out by leadership for their counsel.

- They are skilled at presenting new concepts and have a track record of implementing new technologies (either at the current organization or others if they are new).

- They can be skeptical, as they are detail-oriented.

- More often than not, they own the business problem or outcome.

- They can be passionate, dynamic, and good at convincing others.

We discussed earlier that decisions regarding enterprise solutions are made by groups of people. Finding the key influencer is critical, but they will often look to product and process influencers to support decisions. Even when you have the key influencer on your side, you must still engage the group; group consensus is still critical to success.

Remember that the key influencer is your ally, but you are the one who should be practiced at how to get a decision done. Avoiding the group because you have the key influencer on your side is a really bad idea.

I learned this the hard way. Our team at one of my previous companies was working with a very large organization and we had who we thought was the right executive or key influencer on our side, as he owned the department as well as the budget and was a dynamic leader in the organization.

Each year, our company held a three-day conference in Chicago, inviting existing customers and prospects. We were so confident that we were going to win the deal that we prematurely placed this key influencer on a panel with other existing customers during the event on the main stage. However, he had appointed someone from his team to own the decision process, who was a process influencer.

That person chose one of our competitors over us. Even though we had the key influencer, we were running single-threaded and not engaging the group in an effective way.

Had we partnered with the key influencer more effectively and been more engaged with the decision group, we would have understood the group dynamics and leveraged the key influencer to affect the outcome earlier. The key influencer told us that he had to go with his person's decision since he had appointed him to lead the decision process. Unlike my personal story in the first part of the book with the legendary win for Pyxis, we missed the boat with a critical leading indicator leveraging the key influencer relationship in a strategic way.

The first critical milestone is to identify the key influencer within your targeted account, then leverage the individual as an ally, with the goal of gaining access to the decision group.

Leading A Compelling Discussion With A Differentiated Message

In the sixth edition of *State of Sales* by Salesforce, 59 percent of business buyers say sales representatives don't understand the unique goals they are striving for. The report states, "This perception could indicate that reps aren't doing enough to personalize their communications and show they understand their prospects' unique perspective."[8]

We've all heard the saying that you only get one chance to make a first impression. For this reason, developing a unique, personalized discussion is critical. In fact, when I work with an organization, it is one of the very first projects that I tackle, as uniquely delivering this discussion will attract key influencers.

I like to build a simple slide deck called a "commercial message" that leads the discovery discussion and also delivers insight (see commercial message framework in figure 2). I have found that leading a traditional discovery interrogation is dated and is not aimed at pulling out the providers' unique challenges but rather at asking leading questions for the AE's benefit. A well-crafted commercial message that shows the prospect that you understand their world at a deep level and facilitates an open discussion around strategy as it relates to business outcomes is much more effective. If orchestrated

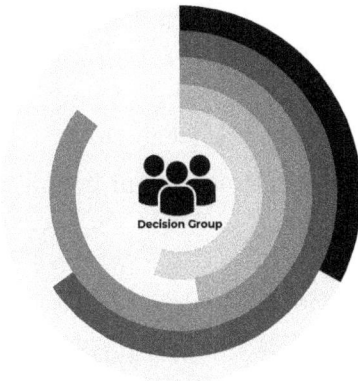

Compelling Thought
- This should be an attention grabber
- It could be stats or a concept that matters deeply to the prospect.

Why It Matters
- How the prospect relates to the concept
- This can be industry challenges or prospect-specific
- Top 3 concept that provokes curiosity

The Strategy "The Money Slide"
- Tells the story of your unique understanding of how to solve the challenges discussed above
- Leads the prospect on a journey to think differently
- NOT a product discussion

Our Solution
- Your product and your edge that ignites the Strategy
- The Strategy discussion should lead to your solution as a "no brainer."

Call To Action
- Leads to a value creation workshop to bring all decision-makers together for consensus building
- Validates that you have the Key Influencer
- If not, CTA should be an introduction to the Key Influencer to present the commercial message

Figure 2

properly, you should create aha moments for the prospect or, at a minimum, get them to think differently and, in turn, differentiate you and your company.

Engaging in this manner makes you unique and unpredictable compared to your competitors. The prospect is not getting the same thirty-two-slide pitch deck that every salesperson who engages with them presents. In my work, 80 percent of the pitch decks I see have the same message—just change the logo—which is all about the company and not the prospect. It doesn't draw them in and make them feel something different.

When I work with my AEs and we review their presentations, I always ask, "If you were in that customer's shoes, would you have paid for that conversation? Because they just did." It is important to do that with every single engagement. You don't have the luxury of being a billion-dollar health tech company that can miss and still win off reputation.

Therefore, the second critical milestone is creating a commercial message delivered through a simple presentation deck that leads discovery and teaches the prospect something unique about their business at the same time.

The Three Whys

I have shared the importance of understanding your company's why. In the buying process, the three whys are all about the customer, their challenges, how much those challenges are costing them, and why you are the perfect fit. It's also a great spot check on qualifying the opportunity throughout the buying process. The three whys are as follows:

Why should the client do something at all? This is the compelling event(s) and exposes their true challenges. The initial phase of uncovering "why do something" starts at discovery with the commercial message and grows as you engage more decision-makers within the organization. It's what makes the opportunity sticky and comes from a deep understanding of the market, what makes your organization unique, and why it matters deeply in a decision.

This is much more than software being sunsetted, so the health system needs to purchase a replacement. This is uncovering the unrealized pain while using the old software and leading them to how your company's solution is best positioned to remove that pain. Anytime you are looking to lead an organization to change, you've always got to be focused on their outcome, not yours. Always remember that if you can't tie a decision in some way to a financial gain, driving change will be nearly impossible.

Why should the client do it now? This is the cost of inaction. There should be a financial impact that creates urgency. The longer they delay, the more the cost of inaction compounds.

A large health system in Houston was looking at buying software to help them negotiate better payer contracts. They were doing a lot of their work on spreadsheets, which was inefficient and extremely time-consuming. Because they couldn't finalize a new contract with new negotiated rates with a particular payer, they were paid with the old rates for three consecutive months. Once they had the new contract in place, they ran the numbers to see what they would have been paid under the new rates. It costs them about a million dollars a month. There is a cost of inaction.

I highly recommend that you build a return-on-investment (ROI) calculator and establish using it early on in your process; it creates credibility for yourself and anchors the deal. It also helps you on the back end when you get into the negotiation. If you agree on a cost of inaction with a prospect, and let's say it's 10X, you can now show the ROI of action with your organization.

Why should it be with us? This involves taking those compelling event(s), establishing their cost, and demonstrating that you are the only company that can solve the issues in a way that benefits the health system. This is where a well-designed business case comes into play. A business case needs to be a well-structured document that you create with your key influencer at the health system to help them sell internally on your behalf.

This will require work on the AE's part, but it is a critical step to get right. This can be simply built in a PowerPoint that includes at a minimum why do something, why now (cost of inaction), why your organization, supporting materials such as case studies, mutual action plan (discussed in a later chapter) with pricing, and high-level implementation.

Depending on the complexity of the product, deal cycle, and number of decision-makers, as well as departments affected by the decision, the complexity of the business case may vary. Still, it must be created within a single document for visibility. We have all made that great presentation and walked away thinking we had the deal done, only to have our key influencer from the health system walk down the hall and be given ten reasons why they shouldn't change. The business case keeps them ready to address internal challenges and helps them sell on your behalf when you're not there.

All opportunities in your pipeline should drive you to take your prospects on a continuous journey to answer and validate these three whys to accelerate the deal.

The third critical milestone to a well-designed buying process is understanding the three whys and tracking them in the CRM over the course of the opportunity.

Power In Numbers

As we've discussed, decisions in enterprise healthcare are almost always made by groups of people. Rarely are they made by individuals alone. One of the biggest mistakes most AEs make is focusing on one person and approaching the opportunity single-threaded. A critical thing you must do with your process is create organizational wins by aligning departments or specialties around desired organizational outcomes. In other words, how will this decision improve the mission and health of the organization as a whole?

The most effective way that I have found to engage the entire decision team all at once is through a whiteboard session. The key to getting buy-in and commitment for the exercise is all in the delivery of the commercial message to the key influencer. Not only do you need to gain a deep understanding of the organization's unique pain and deliver insight, but you also need to share your strategy for solving their unique challenges better than anyone else and how it will deliver a broad organizational impact.

You will notice that I said to share your strategy, not your product. Strategy always comes before product, and when the buy-in on the strategy is executed properly, it will lead to a product discussion. In fact, your strategy should be a natural lead-in for your product being the logical choice.

I have seen on countless occasions when you have the right key influencer and you have an engaging commercial discussion with a buy-in of your company's strategy that aligns with their recognized and hidden challenges, the call to action of bringing the decision group together as a whole works. Because key influencers are focused on performance, as discussed earlier, and carry organizational respect, their ability to make the whiteboard session happen is unmatched.

The goal of the whiteboard session is to create or enhance the business case in a way that, regardless of whether the decision is made to go with your company or not, they will have a blueprint of how to move forward. This takes the business case mentioned earlier to the next level by aligning organizational value and vision around organizational outcomes with a strategy.

Remember, healthcare organizations' missions are very different from those of other businesses. Investing in this milestone early in the process helps you create value for the healthcare organization and demonstrates your willingness to invest in them and not just sell them a product. This process also allows you to qualify the deal further, faster, and more effectively with all of the key decision-makers together at once.

I have an entire framework that I have developed to lead this process (pictured in figure 3). It will allow you to help the decision team sort through all the different data points, break down group dysfunction, and create group consensus. This is one of the most effective and critical milestones to ensuring a winning decision I have ever coached. In fact, when gaining a commitment to include the whiteboard in the decision process and when we get the right group of people together, I have seen a 90 percent win rate.

I know that with the rise in remote workers, bringing the entire decision group together to an onsite location can be a challenge. However, with the technology that is available through video conference apps and virtual whiteboards, the process is still possible and game changing.

Whiteboard & Business Case Creation

Figure 3

The fourth critical milestone is gaining access to the decision group by leveraging the key influencer, creating group consensus, and focusing on workshopping value creation first before a detailed product demonstration.

Putting Process Into Action

I was the CRO for a small health tech company. We were pursuing one of the largest health systems in the country, and we knew that we were up against a billion-dollar private equity-backed company.

It was clear from our initial meeting with the health system that we had the key influencer. He was an executive who led the functional areas within the finance department that we had determined aligned best with our solution, even though our solutions could affect the entire department. Our commercial message really resonated with him, and he saw how our integrated solution would not only affect his functional area but also meet the needs of the entire finance department and align with the overall strategic vision of the health system.

He committed to bringing the rest of his team and the other functions within finance together to complete a whiteboard discussion. The day of the whiteboard session came, and we had a room full of people. We began working our process. Everyone was a little quiet to begin with because this was a different approach from our competitor and from anything they had experienced in the past.

After an hour into the discussion, the key influencer left the room to pull in one of the senior executives because of the value he saw in the process. As we finished the session and people were leaving the room, they were actually taking pictures of the whiteboard with their smartphones. This has become so common that when I do in-person whiteboard sessions, I always know if we hit the mark when participants take a picture of the work we created together as they exit.

Next, we huddled internally and designed the business case from the whiteboard session. We then presented a very focused demo that brought to life the strategy that we had cocreated with their team in the whiteboard session.

They came back and said, "We love what we're hearing from you guys, but we need to follow the procurement process because we are a nonprofit organization, so we need to issue a request for proposal—an RFP." When we received the RFP, a lot of our strategy from the commercial discussions, the three whys, the business case components from the whiteboard session that we had designed with their team, and the integrated offering that we demoed were lockout specs (specifications that only our solution could solve) in the RFP. We had included a mutual action plan in the business case (tasks and timelines that mutually need to be completed prior to going live), and our timetable from the plan was identical to the RFP dates.

Not only did the RFP appear to be in our favor, but our key influencer was coaching us on how to proceed. This is a key point as I see too often where an AE's perceived champion states they want to "play fair" with all competitors in the process. Guess what? That individual might be a key influencer, but they're not yours. We've all won deals where this is the case, but I have lost them more often than not. How your key influencer treats you throughout the process is a clear sign of a truly qualified opportunity and whether they are a true ally.

We won the opportunity, and it was the largest deal in the history of that health tech company at the time and became the jumping-off point for the predictable growth of the organization.

After the deal was done, I went to dinner with the key influencer, and I asked him what was the biggest reason for choosing us. He told me that we helped them make a decision, while they felt that our competitor was just trying to sell them. He didn't say that we won because of product, price, or brand. To put it a different way, we won because of the buying experience that we created for the health system. That was music to my ears.

What we did was literally guide them through the purchase process. By leading the purchase experience in this way, you are demonstrating how you will treat the organization post-sale. This develops respect and trust for your company. I've also found that it will help increase the velocity of the decision process.

As a startup or scaleup, you don't have the luxury of leaning on your brand. You must have a repeatable, predictable internal process so that you can be unpredictable and uncommon—in a good way—to your prospects.

Keep in mind that most of these folks have never made decisions like this before, or they have only done it once or twice over the course of their careers. The bottom line is that you are more experienced at this than they are, and you should show that you have a repeatable process to lead them to a good decision.

Yes, you can certainly wing it every time or go to the same pitch deck and demo and hope for the best. Or, you can provide a proven approach to help your prospect make the best decision and lean on you as the trusted advisor.

Now that you have developed your why, who you should be targeting, and how you will execute a sound buying process, you have the foundation for efficiently approaching the market to build a qualified pipeline.

Three Takeaways

1 Clearly and succinctly define your why and what makes your organization unique. Get everyone on the same page and pressure test everything you do against it.

2 Take a deep dive into your TAM, break down your service addressable market, and identify your ICP with target personas. Determine what a qualified and unqualified target looks like. Leverage data or do it manually. It's that important.

3 Design a buying process that is a step-by-step strategy on how to effectively win in your ICP. Build it out within your CRM, targeting nonnegotiable milestones such as engaging the key influencer, creating a guided commercial message instead of a sales pitch deck, uncovering the three whys, and engaging with the decision group to create value and drive group consensus.

4

Stone Two:
Pipeline

ichard Branson famously said, "Business opportunities are like buses; there's always another one coming." No offense to Mr. Branson, but that's not the case in enterprise healthcare. Opportunities don't just show up, especially when you are a startup or scaleup struggling to build a qualified pipeline.

A healthy pipeline is a leading indicator of a healthy go-to-market strategy. If you don't have revenue, you don't have a business. If you don't have a pipeline, you don't have a business either, because you'll never generate revenue. I have seen so many organizations that say they have a lead-generation problem; however, I would argue that they really have a pipeline strategy problem.

Don't get me wrong; leads are important, and you might argue, "What's the difference?" Just like creating your organization's why and what makes you unique, it's a matter of perspective. You, as the leader, need to set the correct expectations for optimal performance. If everyone on your go-to-market team is not aligned on growing the pipeline as the top priority next to closing deals, you need to fix it.

Best Framework For Qualifying Your Pipeline

Building a real, qualified pipeline is a top priority for any smaller company looking to scale. It's your lifeblood.

It's equally important to have a clearly defined way for everyone in the organization to know what makes a deal in the pipeline qualified. I've used BANT (budget, authority, need, and timing) before, as well as other systems of collected data points, but as an example, timing and budget aren't always clearly defined in early-stage deals and are shaped during the buying process. That is why it is so important to clearly define an end-to-end buying process because a collection of important data points does not tell the entire story or provide context in a strategic way to understand succinctly how the opportunity is tracking in the beginning, middle, and near the end.

As mentioned in the previous chapter, having a tight alignment with your SAM is critical to a solid pipeline-building strategy. A smaller player just simply doesn't have the budget to throw money at guessing about pipeline targeting and throwing random programs and campaigns against the wall to see what sticks.

Getting your TAM, SAM, ICP, and go-to-market buying process right will help you make decisions on which pipeline strategies will work best for your organization and drive greater efficiencies in the execution of those decisions. Not only is not getting this right a recipe for disaster, but it is also one of the biggest hidden factors for the slow death of a company.

The Most Effective Ways To Drive Pipeline

In Chet Holmes's 2007 book, *The Ultimate Sales Machine*, he introduced the buyer's pyramid.[9] The concept of the pyramid pictured in figure 4 is still relevant today.

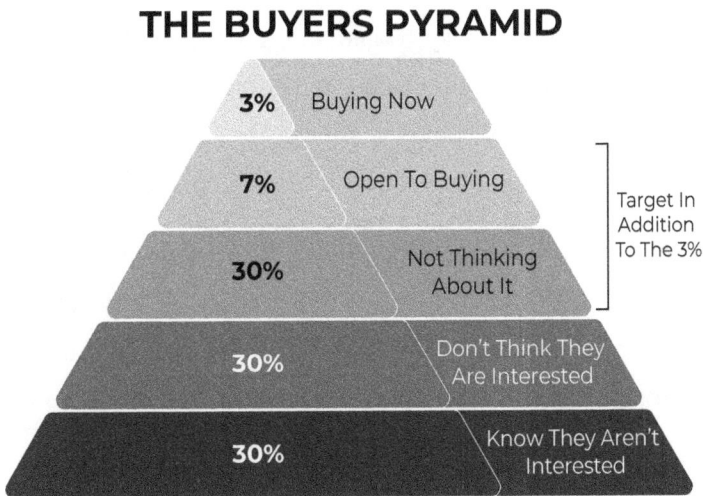

THE BUYERS PYRAMID

3%	Buying Now
7%	Open To Buying
30%	Not Thinking About It
30%	Don't Think They Are Interested
30%	Know They Aren't Interested

Target In Addition To The 3%

Chet Holmes, *The Ultimate Sales Machine*

Figure 4

Every pipeline strategy of every competitor in your market is focused on the top 3 percent. Those are the prospects who are raising their hands and whom your competitors are leveraging everything at their disposal to attract. Obviously, the 3 percent is important, but you must expand your reach with your strategy to connect with the 7 percent open to change and the next third who might be open but are currently neutral.

What different levers can you pull early in your growth to attract prospects in the top three tiers of the pyramid and drive a qualified pipeline? It should never be single-threaded as it needs to be an omnichannel approach. Here are the top pipeline-generating strategies I have found most effective that can work together to drive a healthy pipeline.

Referrals

There is no better way to generate pipeline than a warm referral. My greatest success from referrals always comes from existing customers, clients who have had success and moved to new accounts, and personal networks from our employees.

Referrals should be a top priority for the customer success team or customer support. If you are in the early startup stage and don't have a large client base, marketing should be accessing the entire team's LinkedIn connections to bump against targeted ICPs and gain warm introductions.

In addition, AEs need to have an intentional referral strategy. I had an individual on one of my teams who was so dialed into our market that almost all of his business came through referrals. Find those individuals within your market who have those types of connections and hire them immediately!

This team member understood that referrals are like any other relationship and that they need to be nurtured. He had a strategy of not just reaching out to remind them that he was there, but also to support them. He would share intel on the industry and check in on how they were navigating their role in their organization. It wasn't a sales or prospecting call, but it often turned into one.

As referrals moved from organization to organization, he leveraged these relationships to introduce him to new healthcare facilities, and his network expanded exponentially over the years. That investment has paid dividends for this individual for many years.

LinkedIn must be a priority, and adding LinkedIn Sales Navigator, which provides contact access to the over one billion worldwide professionals on the site, should be an important investment in your tech stack. The individual above looked upon LinkedIn like a personal CRM, where he shared his area of expertise with his network and could see in a nonintrusive fashion what his connections were up to.

Channel Partnerships

A pipeline miss I see with startups and scaleups is failing to leverage partnership channel programs. Channel partnerships are designed to scale an organization and gain market share at a lower acquisition cost. It's a one-to-many relationship. Over time, it will ramp up and you will see a velocity that you wouldn't normally be able to accomplish through direct sales alone.

That's not to say that channel partnerships are a replacement for direct sales. They help your revenue ramp-up go faster because they provide the credibility you may lack as a startup. Selecting strategic partners that already have a strong presence in the market with a solid client list gives you instant credibility.

It's important to do proper due diligence to determine who the optimal strategic partners should be. Select ones that are a seamless fit and, together with you, will enhance value. This is not a numbers game. I have seen companies sign up a laundry list of partners with poor overall results. Pick quality over quantity.

Here are a few examples of partnerships that my teams have formed that have helped increase credibility, seamlessly fit together for increased value, and have grown pipeline. We have worked with banking institutions that have strong relationships with healthcare systems and helped us promote our patient-payment software. We have also partnered with an electronic medical record vendor and leveraged our patient-engagement platform to communicate more effectively with the patients that their clients serve. These partners had relationships and access to accounts that would have taken years for us alone to develop, if at all.

A key component of the channel partnership program is to create incentives that help a partner have the same goals as you—to gain market share. This includes a referral model, revenue share model, and reseller model.

Let's take a quick look at those three most effective models.

Referral Model

In this model, less training is required of the channel partner. You are simply looking for a warm introduction and the partner is paid for that lead. This is easier to scale with less complication and contracting, and is an easy way to get your feet wet with a partner program.

Revenue Share Model

This is more than a referral, and usually, the partner is more involved in the entire buying process, as they will receive a portion of the revenue for the life of the agreement. The contract with the client is most often still on your paper, but because the partner is sharing in the revenue, they are more involved during the life of the agreement.

This model can be beneficial to help with customer success, support challenges, and upsell/cross-sell opportunities down the road. From a coverage perspective, your AEs will usually sell shoulder-to-shoulder with the partner company's AEs.

It's extremely important that incentive plans are aligned to drive prioritization of your solution, and it's important that your AEs take on an active role in managing the local relationship with the partner AE.

Reseller Model

This option brings the most value over time. When the reseller is selling your product, you are truly adding to your sales team by the number of sellers the partner company has. And your solution is truly a value added to their core offering.

Because the partner company will require more comprehensive training, the ramp to revenue will be slower than referral or revenue sharing. Your AEs will often function as subject matter experts (SMEs) to the reseller's AEs. As with revenue sharing, compensation must be aligned to drive performance and bookings. The reseller model also requires the most hands-on partnership management to ensure your product is a priority to the reseller. In addition, other decisions will need to be made around who owns implementation and support, which could add another layer of required training.

Regardless of the flavor of channel program you chose, or if you choose to incorporate all three, this pipeline lever will uncover opportunities in the market that you were not aware existed. However, to make them effective, it's important to enable your partner to sell on your behalf and to ensure incentives are aligned to make your company a priority. This includes proper marketing and training. It's also important that your sales team takes an active role in managing the partnership in their given geography or territories and that it is being coached and managed continuously.

Sales Development Reps (SDRs)

SDR teams that I have built over my career have delivered on some of the largest pipeline opportunities that I've seen.

The mistake that I see with most SDR teams is that they are simply handed a call list and generic scripts and told to go at it. That path lacks a standardized approach with results similar to the lack of a buying process with the sales team. The most common argument that I hear against an SDR team is that people are just not answering the phones anymore which makes them less effective at engaging prospects. The dials should only be one aspect of the SDR process. This is where a more comprehensive strategy comes into play.

The lack of strategy starts with only targeting or bombarding the individual considered to be the key influencer with phone calls, emails, and social media messaging. When this leads to very poor conversion rates, additional messages are often developed to target other potential influencers within the organization or the key influencer with a completely different storyline.

Logically, this might make sense, but in practice, it rarely works. I have found that it is much more effective to build one message that is important to the key influencer and that will resonate across the entire organization. By doing this, instead of targeting one individual, you broaden the scope of influence and target the entire organization's leadership.

This singular messaging and top-down approach create social awareness throughout the healthcare organization. It can lead to being top of mind during water cooler discussions, leadership meetings, or even catching the attention of a CEO who is losing sleep over the organization's problems that your company is uniquely equipped to solve.

When it comes to hiring and managing the SDR team, having a repeatable process, as I've outlined, enables you to compare each team member, as everyone is operating within the same framework. The various touchpoints in the process will provide leading indicators or milestones, just as you have with a well-orchestrated buying process with the sales team.

Having a repeatable process will also help you to create the correct hiring profile.

If your company does not have the budget to hire an SDR team, this strategy should be at the core of your AE's outbound prospecting strategy. If you are looking to build an SDR team for the first time, begin with at least two so that you can gamify the process and create healthy competition to fuel your outbound strategy.

SDRs In Action

Everywhere that I have implemented this approach of creating social awareness with a single message with the SDR team, I have seen dramatic improvements in meetings held and pipeline generated. In my most recent experience with a five-person SDR team, we saw meetings double and a 165 percent increase in pipeline the following month solely attributed to the SDR team. These results are common when the system is implemented and executed properly.

Here is a story of my first encounter with the process of creating social awareness as an executive on the prospect side of the equation. I was having pipeline issues at one of my companies. The SDR process company that I now use as the basis for all SDR teams reached out to my CEO and CFO, spoke to our executive assistant every three days, left me messages and emails, and reached out to me via LinkedIn.

My CEO forwarded me an email that was sent to him and asked if we should be talking to this company. During our next Monday morning leadership meeting, we discussed our pipeline, and this organization was brought up again during the leadership meeting. Even the CFO mentioned that they had been communicating with him as well.

They engaged every key person in our organization with the same consistent message about how they solve pipeline challenges uniquely, and they were persistent. I ended up calling the company, and we signed a contract to implement their system.

Studies have shown that it takes between three and seven outreaches to get a prospect to engage. Most salespeople quit after just one. These guys obviously did not and leveraged a systemic process to engage. No one in our company picked up a single one of their calls, but they created a buzz within our organization because they hit a nerve on a challenge that I owned as the CRO, which was also affecting the entire company and hindering our growth.

Marketing

I am not here claiming to be a marketing guru, and that is why one of my most important first hires has always been a scrappy marketing leader. I want to share strategies that I have found deliver the greatest ROI, which is what boards, investors, leadership teams, and you, as the company leader, should care about the most. This book is about how to compete differently to scale your business, so I want to focus on the most cost-effective ways to see the fastest impact on pipeline.

In most organizations I have led, we have looked at high-touch marketing strategies to begin and then evolved to expand into a one-to-many approach and paid marketing.

The first step is to know your numbers. We will discuss the math behind broader go-to-market decisions in a later chapter, but specifically for marketing, the question is how to evaluate the marketing team's success in enterprise pipeline generation and conversion.

Example: Marketing Target Metrics To Validate Campaign Success

Revenue/Booking Target	Deals Required
$R = ACV \times Deals$	$D = Opportunities \times Conversion\ Rate$

Opportunities Required
$O = Lead \times Conversion\ Rate$

Assuming:	Key Results:
12-Month Revenue/Booking Objective = $10M	Total Deals = 20
Average ACV = $500k	Opportunities = 80
Opportunity Conversion Rate = .25	Leads = 533
Lead To Oppty Conversion Rate = .15	

Figure 5

It all should start by creating a marketing revenue or bookings goal. To do this, you simply take your average contract value (ACV) times the number of deals required to make your revenue or bookings target. From there, you determine how many opportunities you would need to close to achieve your targeted revenue/bookings by taking the number of opportunities times your conversation rate. Finally, you take leads required times your lead conversion rate to project how many opportunities you will need to add to the pipeline. These are not marketing vanity metrics but breaking down the marketing engagements to how you will drive and measure true results.

Once you have determined your high-level targets, the final step is to break them down by each of your individual marketing strategies over a given time period, using the same metrics of bookings/revenue target, opportunities or pipeline required, and leads needed to convert.

Top High-Touch Marketing Strategies To Drive Pipeline The Fastest

Content

As with all marketing activities, any high-touch strategy begins by creating great content and knowing how and when to deliver it to your ICP. Within health tech, specifically enterprise accounts, developing a comprehensive approach that catches a prospect's attention and causes them to raise their hand is the first basic step to creating a solid content strategy.

Most organizations that I have worked with all have subject matter experts and should be your first source for building your content calendar, not outsourced agencies. With the AI tools available on the market, leveraging SME knowledge to convert to compelling content has been made much easier. The next step is simply getting the content into the hands of key influencers who care about it to help educate and/or deliver insight that gets them thinking and wanting to learn more.

Additionally, creating a "thought followship" program by leveraging existing customers to produce testimonials, case studies, video content, and webinars is important, which we will discuss later in this chapter. Just like with key influencers in the buying process, no one can sell your solutions more effectively than your ICP's peers. Leveraging these relationships strategically by creating insightful content that leads prospects to follow you is highly effective as a startup or scaleup.

Building compelling content enables your organization to engage with accounts that matter.

Account-Based Marketing

I have found a solid ABM program to be a highly effective, high-touch strategy. Again, this goes back to creating the right content for the top of the funnel to create awareness and then throughout the funnel to drive engagement with the buyer at multiple steps in the buyer's journey.

When you invest in this marketing strategy, it's critical that the goal is to take it beyond traditional thought leadership to deliver unique insight. When executed properly, you can help your prospects internalize what makes you different and how you are uncommon from your competitors. And what makes you uncommon and unpredictable can make you quite interesting.

My head of marketing came to me one day and said that the next new piece of content would be about our competition. I was taken aback because that is a topic go-to-market teams have always been told to avoid. My head of marketing shared with me that he had attended a conference and that there are five questions that every buyer asks.

If you write content on these five questions, you can see your organic search skyrocket. We chose to write on one of those as a test. Sure enough, when we wrote a competitive analysis, our content ranked higher than any of our competitors when searching for vendors in our space, even by specific names.

This strategy didn't require expensive Google Ads or outsourcing to an agency. It required confidence in our understanding of the space and what makes us unique. As a footnote, I'm not here to discourage engaging with an agency, as I have found success in doing so. I am saying that it's not required in the early stages of your growth if you do not have the budget. However, it can be advantageous as you scale to help follow your ICPs around the internet and enhance your multi-touch attribution strategy.

The Big 5™ questions you should answer in business blog:

1. Price and cost?
Explain cost and pricing—and what factors make those numbers go up or down.

2. Problems?
Be open about the problems, shortcomings, and drawbacks of what you sell.

3. Versus and comparisons?
Compare several products or services so the buyer can understand the differences.

4. Reviews?
Produce "best of" lists that cover best in class, best practices, and more.

5. Best in class?
Create (or collect) helpful reviews from experts and past customers.

—*They Ask, You Answer*, by Marcus Sheridan

A great example of an ABM strategy occurred while attending a meeting with a new prospect. A key executive came into the room and said, "I know you guys. I've read a lot of your content, and you helped educate me on the problem we are trying to address." As mentioned earlier, we leveraged our SMEs and client base to build compelling content, and as a result, we created thought followship with that key executive.

That's when you know that you are making an impact with your content and marketing. You don't have to be a large organization to be able to do that. As a matter of fact, a lot of the content that I see in the market is not compelling. I think that's because it can be a really hard thing to do when you do not have a relentless focus to be compelling to your ICP.

At one of my organizations, we created a formula—the formula is insight plus revelation equals change. What I see most often is when people are developing content, they report the news. It's a marketing person, not a subject matter expert writing it.

They outsourced the content creation to someone who does not understand the market, and they developed really fluffy content that reads pretty but has no impact. If you report the news, you waste the reader's time. When you write good content and practice thought leadership, you become credible. With credibility comes customer engagement. But that's still not enough, as Goliaths can be good at creating thought leadership with their larger, more well-funded marketing teams.

Insight + Revelation = *Change*

Report | Thought Leadership | Insight | Change | Revelation | Credible | Waste

The News   Strategy   Client Time

Figure 6

As the formula says, you must deliver insight. This is content that gets the client thinking differently. When you hit this sweet spot, you can take the prospect's mind to a place it has never been before, which creates a revelation that drives change.

Your marketing department must be writing content that delivers insight. We are striving for the reader to say, "Wow, these guys see my problem differently. They understand me. I've never really thought about it like that before."

This is not about creating content simply to do so or solely as a lead magnet. This is about creating value and conversation with your content and building that relationship so that when the time comes, the prospect knows who to call because you already have invested with them.

Trade Shows

Every organization I've worked with has questioned the high-touch marketing strategy of trade shows. It typically comes down to strategy and focus as it relates to a good experience or a bad one. It all begins with focusing on shows that matter and which ones have the greatest opportunity to engage with ICP prospects.

Once you understand which ones present the greatest opportunities, you must develop a comprehensive strategy for attracting and managing booth traffic and, equally important, how you engage with prospects outside of the booth. In addition, you must build metrics, as mentioned earlier, that start months before the show to drive your targeting.

An extremely effective strategy that I've used is to place a production crew in the booth to film interviews with thought leaders at the conference and then post them on social media. This drives heavy views and shares and drives impressions through the roof. It also creates a buzz on the tradeshow floor and attracts booth traffic. If you use this strategy, it's important to take it past vanity metrics and track conversion rates to closed business just like any other marketing initiative, as this is a great thought followship program. In addition, I highly recommend having your SMEs speak at conferences to drive brand awareness and leads.

Regardless of what you do, every minute of the show should have meaning and purpose. Also, everyone from your company in attendance must be coached on a strategy for engaging prospects when they are not on the exhibitor floor. This isn't a vacation, and it should not be treated like one.

Webinars

Webinars are a great way to build content, create thought leadership, and deliver insight to the marketplace. They are also the perfect way to engage with your ICP, expand your prospect list, and add to your community of thought followers. Creating thought followership with webinars means that the content must be focused on solving problems for your ICP, not pitching a product.

The best way to start a webinar strategy is to work with media influencers in the healthcare industry, such as Becker's Healthcare. Organizations like Becker's have access to healthcare leaders as they are known for providing information, analytics, and guidance to these key individuals. Much like channel partners, they will have the ear of a large majority of healthcare organizations and can accelerate access. It can be pricey, but these respected media channels will ensure a certain number of attendees, and they can become strategic partners early in your growth. In addition to media influencers, other national associations and accrediting bodies will also sponsor webinars for educational purposes to gain access.

Another effective way to leverage webinars is in collaboration with your channel partners. When performed properly, both you and your channel partner can deliver insight into the market and demonstrate how an integrated approach between the two organizations can benefit the prospect. It can also lend to your credibility by aligning with a more recognized market ally.

Finally, webinars can be an effective tool in your organization's account-based marketing strategy. Regardless of where the prospect is in the buyer's journey, educating your prospect and delivering insight will only increase your credibility.

ICP Engagement Events

This is where you create your own event and invite a combination of existing customers and prospects to a dinner with an industry-expert speaker or a fun, engaging activity. These events are usually regional for travel purposes and help build a specific territory pipeline.

With one of my previous companies, we sponsored a driving experience at the Charlotte Motor Speedway, where we had a few existing clients and twenty prospects attend the event. Each participant was able to drive two exotic cars around the road course. The experience was incredibly exciting and led to some amazing bonding between the entire group. We concluded the event with a lunch and had an existing client speak to the group. This was not a "sales presentation," but we eventually won three opportunities from the event, which made the cost to put it on a fraction of the generated revenue.

Customer Success—Upsell/Cross-Sell Into The Existing Base

In general, most businesses see greater revenue by selling into existing customers than to new ones. However, startups and scaleups might not have the customer base to move the needle on upsell/cross-sell opportunities. Upsell/cross-sell opportunities obviously depend a great deal on product and pricing models (subscription, usage-based, bundled versus unbundled, etc.), in addition to installed base.

Customer success strategies could fill another book for another time, but to simplify for the purpose of pipeline and revenue growth, let's take a look at a few key metrics. Logo retention (how many logos I have and how effective I am at maintaining them) and gross revenue retention (how I am retaining my core revenue streams from each existing customer minus expansion) are important metrics to run the business. However, understanding your net revenue retention (revenue by client plus expansion minus churn) becomes the pipeline driver for upsell/cross-sell.

Obviously, the higher the opportunity number is above 100 percent, the healthier your cross-sell/upsell and customer retention strategy is. Depending on your product and pricing model, completing a white-space analysis on each client can provide quick gains in pipeline and revenue. This should be a continuous process starting early in the company's growth as an important part of the go-to-market strategy.

Determining When You Have Enough Pipeline

Understanding the required amount of pipeline to hit the annual bookings number depends on several metrics. Win rate helps you to understand how much and how often you close deals in the pipeline. Deal size is also important as well as the average time it takes to close/convert a deal or the average sales cycle.

Most companies that I work with do not have access to these metrics as they have rarely trended pipeline data or they have recently implemented a CRM and don't have historical data. In either case, a good rule of thumb is to start with three times the quota as a target and then build from there. However, it is critical that once you have an omnichannel pipeline strategy in place, you create a pipeline dashboard and start to track these basic metrics, as well as stage duration, milestone adherence, and others.

When you get the right processes in place by working referrals strategically, developing targeted partner programs, creating a cold-outreach strategy with your SDRs, implementing high-touch marketing initiatives, and creating the right buzz in the market by delivering true insight, you will start to see pipeline momentum in a big way.

From my very first CRO role, where we saw qualified pipeline quickly grow to a five-times multiple, to my most recent engagement, where we saw a pipeline increase by 240 percent within the first two quarters, an omnichannel approach to pipeline build was a game changer. It can be for your organization as well.

An Example Of Omnichannel Excellence

Leveraging an omnichannel approach to pipeline build is critical, but leveraging it to help opportunities convert is equally as important.

Our SDR team started reaching out to attendees of targeted accounts before an upcoming conference to book meetings. One of our AEs met during the conference with a potential client who stopped by the booth because of the SDR's outreach.

The prospect did show a lot of interest, so the AE booked a follow-up meeting after the conference. After several meetings and following our buying process, the prospect let us know that their organization had some internal conversations and, due to budget challenges, they could not move forward at this time.

We put the potential client into an account-based marketing sequence and delivered tailored content to different members of the buying committee. After a few months, we sponsored a webinar, which several members of the organization attended.

We followed up with each attendee from the organization, but we were cautious not to be intrusive as they were still a few months from the beginning of their fiscal year.

A few more months went by, and in addition to the account-based marketing strategy, our SDR team started re-engaging with the potential client as they approached the beginning of their new fiscal year. We booked a meeting, and the AE re-engaged in the buying process as the entire buying committee was ready to move forward.

All touch points helped educate the prospect on what made us different from our competitors with a consistent message around our why and how our unique differences aligned to their specific challenges. This made us the perfect partner for this prospect, and we booked the deal. By staying engaged with the potential client, we kept the deal in play, but it took more than one approach to do so. We stayed front and center without overstepping and remained passively engaged until the potential client was ready to move forward. You may call it multi-touch attribution for marketing metrics and measurement sake, but the bottom line is that it works.

In all of these approaches, you need to constantly pressure test to make sure you are delivering insight that's driving the revelation. That is the only way you're going to get over the inertia of not making a decision and avoiding change.

Now with a solid buying process and pipeline strategy in place, you can move to becoming internally predictable.

Three Takeaways

1 Start thinking of all outbound and inbound activities with a pipeline-first mentality.

2 Once you have developed your buying process and created fields for each milestone in your CRM, start using it to qualify your opportunities. Also, pipeline goals should be set and tracked in the CRM.

3 Evaluate your pipeline activities to determine if you have an integrated, omnichannel approach to pipeline build. Do you have a strategy for referrals in place? Could a partner program benefit your organization? Is there a systemic approach to outbound (SDRs)? Is your marketing team optimizing high-touch activities to build pipeline? And how are you measuring all of your pipeline activities to ensure you optimize your investments?

5

Stone Three: Predictability

Simon Sinek once said, "Always plan for the fact that no plan goes according to plan." However, the stronger your leading indicators are, the less likely your plan will be to fly off the rails and rely on hope instead of predictability.

When I am working with an organization on how to manage stone three of predictability, in every situation where I see weak forecasting, it always involves a lack of clarity around the pipeline and its integration into the buying process.

As we discussed when we kicked off examining the 5 Stone Growth Systems, sequence matters. Developing a repeated buying process grounded in the strategy that leads a client to make a decision is the critical first step to creating an accurate forecast model. Documenting the buying process sequentially in the CRM not only enables the inspection of a qualified pipeline but also opens up accuracy with your forecasting through the shorthand language it creates during opportunity reviews.

As a result, if an organization is truly committed to its buying process and follows it starting in the earlier stages, committing deals becomes a believable system for managing predictable bookings.

Affecting Predictability With Commits And Best Case Deals

If you have ever managed a forecast model where you require AEs to commit opportunities so that you can forecast bookings and, ultimately, revenue, you know AEs typically fall into two camps: those who will not commit anything and those who overcommit everything.

I've beaten this horse to death, but why stop now? A repeatable buying process that is tracked in your CRM can change the paradigm and pull the two commitment extremes to the center. It answers the question of why a particular deal should be committed and why others should not. As you dial in the buying process stages and align milestones toward a closing strategy, probability and hard close dates will become clearer.

Buy-in and adherence to the process should be nonnegotiable. The standardized shorthand language is the only conversation that should happen during the weekly forecast review with the team. Even so, sometimes opportunities do occasionally slip, and there should be some degree of variation in the forecast that is allowed, but it needs to be minimal.

Commits

To start, these are the opportunities with an 80 percent certainty that the opportunity will close by the forecast date in the CRM. Early on, this may be a little more about feel but should quickly evolve into more of a math problem once you have a better understanding of how you can lead the buying decision with the buying process. With better data and practice, I move this to a 90 percent probability or greater. The old-school way of thinking is to ask, "Would you commit the deal in blood?" We'll get to a "blood" commitment once we have the support driven by data from the buying process, but you need to crawl with commits before you run.

Best Case

These are the air-cover opportunities for the approximately 20 percent of commits that have the potential to slip. These are the deals for which you have a minimum 50 percent chance of closing by the close date listed in the CRM. Best-case opportunities are deals that are tracking well but may have certain challenges with timing. However, they should never lack any of the early steps of qualification or value creation.

Weekly Forecast Meeting

Most organizations have a weekly check-in on deals, which often turns into a weekly storytelling exercise with maybe a few new details. The AE starts by sharing much of the same points that you heard last week with slightly more information. This often turns the meeting into an unstructured call that runs over the allotted time, and no one benefits from a learning perspective. It's up to you or your revenue leader to pull out what's new and how the opportunity has advanced since last week.

In contrast, when the weekly check-in is reported directly from the CRM with the succinct strategy sequenced to the buying process and the critical milestones, the meeting changes to a shorthand discussion of what has changed and how the AE can be supported to advance the buying strategy. Structuring the call this way reduces noise to focus on the facts in the deal review and creates a coaching opportunity across the board on the buying process adoption.

To guide the discussion during the weekly forecast meeting, I build a dashboard in the CRM that looks at four metrics (4Ps) in real time (aligning with the first four stones):

Performance To Quota	Pipeline	Predictability	Process
How are the AEs tracking toward their number?	Are they building enough pipeline to hit their quotas (typically three times their quota as a rule of thumb until we have better data on win rates, etc.)?	Do they have enough commits/best cases to cover their quota?	As we've discussed, because we document the buying process the way we do in the CRM, we can now move the process from being subjective to objective.

These four metrics can quickly tell you the health of an AE's business.

I have found this method of forecasting, which is tied tightly to the buying process, to be extremely effective in helping right-fit AEs manage their business. Conversations about poor process adoption and poor forecasting aren't fun, but necessary. In early-stage companies, you need to identify poor performance quickly and take corrective action.

A Not-So-Fun Situation

I had an AE who had that one big deal in his pipeline and nothing else of significance. When we looked at the 4Ps dashboard from week to week during the team forecast calls, he wasn't building pipeline; he only had the one committed opportunity he discussed each week that wasn't progressing.

With this individual, there were rarely notes on the milestones for any of his opportunities that we had laid out as a team in the CRM or any indication that he was following the process other than lip service. We've all heard the saying that if it's not in the CRM, it didn't happen. In this case, he wasn't willing to get outside his comfort zone to internalize and work the process. This caused him to stick out during the weekly forecast meetings in a bad way. In addition, he hadn't closed anything of significance in multiple quarters. And so, I had to have that difficult conversation with him.

My conversation with him went as follows: "Put yourself in my shoes, and you are having this conversation with someone chasing that one big deal with nothing else in the pipeline to speak of. Their pipeline is not growing, so there is no path to hitting their quota outside of this one big deal that we've been talking about for weeks.

"Additionally, this person missed their quota last quarter and it's clear that if that one big deal doesn't come in, they're going to miss this quarter. Because they don't have any pipeline to speak of even if that one big deal comes in, we will probably be sitting in the same situation in a few weeks from now. On top of all of that, there is no documentation of the buying process in the CRM, which means there is no commitment to working our winning strategy. What does that say about this individual's business? Is it healthy or unhealthy? What would you do?"

This spotlights how the AE manages their business as a whole. When measured properly, the data helps you make tough decisions rather than making it about feel.

It also helps you preserve the winning culture as everyone is clear on the standards that are expected, and everyone is held to the same level of performance and predictability. Needless to say, he didn't last long in that role, but there was very little pushback because the data was clear. I am far from a punitive leader. I want to focus on positive momentum, and this methodology has allowed me to let the metrics handle the difficult conversation. Hence, the team as a whole remains positive and in growth mode.

In addition to the weekly forecast meeting, I usually have two other kinds of touchpoints with the sales team during the week.

I have a daily stand-up called the BMC huddle, which stands for build, move, close. The BMC huddle is daily except on the day of the weekly forecast meeting. This is a succinct twenty-minute call at a standard scheduled time where each AE gets on and *only* calls out pipeline *build* from the previous day, any opportunity that made a significant *move* either from a stage or overcoming a key milestone within a stage, and any opportunity that *closed*.

I had one of my very best AEs tell me once that when I introduced the BMC huddle that she hated it. Every day when she would get on the check-in call, it would be uncomfortable if several days had gone by where there was nothing to report. However, she did confide that it eventually helped instill a sense of urgency and new habits that helped lead her to greater success in managing her business.

I have found it's also important to have weekly one-on-one meetings with each AE to provide time for them to touch base with me on any challenges they are dealing with, early-stage deals, or wants and needs from pipeline build to operational problems they might be experiencing.

Finally, I hold a virtual or in-person QBR (Quarter Business Review), which is a more in-depth view of the weekly forecast meeting where each AE has an hour to look back at the previous quarter and year-to-date performance with a look forward at the next two quarters. Once again, we use the 4Ps dashboard to analyze performance, pipeline, predictability, and process. This is a health-of-the-territory check-in, and I leverage the previous QBR 4Ps data to reflect on how well each AE performed based on their numbers and commits. I also leverage the time together for training and allowing each AE to share their thoughts on additional support needed to succeed and review progress on any OKRs and team initiatives.

Preventing Opportunities From Pushing

We've all experienced it. Deals push. This can be painful even when you believe you have done everything right. For this reason, an important thing to religiously validate is the client's internal process for approval before, during, and after a verbal commitment. For example, what's the redline process that the organization needs to go through? Do you truly understand their sign-off process, and does it require board approval? When does the board meet, who signs, and how many signatures are required? This always has an impact on predictability and performance.

I highly recommend that, as part of your buying process, you create a mutual action plan document that aligns all the activities required by both parties to reach a signed contract. This is where you partner with your key influencer within the health system to understand when the deal is going to get done and how. It should also outline your company's internal process with timing. As an example, implementation and training resources could affect the go-live from your perspective. The targeted go-live date functions as the end date for what is basically a reverse timeline for the project.

Coupled with the mutual action plan, a great way to create urgency is to anchor the opportunity with the cost of inaction. As a reminder, the cost of inaction is one of the three whys. This illustrates how much the health system is losing each month the go-live is delayed.

I think we've all seen it in the CRM—every deal will close on June 30 or August 31. And boy, we're going to have an amazing celebration on August 31 because we will bring in all this business. When the deal slips, that has a huge impact on performance. A mutual action plan provides more concrete data on when the deal will close and go live (go to www.5stonesgrowth.com/tools to download a free mutual action plan template).

Now that you understand the value of a comprehensive buying process, how to build a qualified pipeline, and how to make it predictable, it is time to start seeing scalable performance for ultimate shareholder value.

Three Takeaways

1 Build the 4Ps dashboard in the CRM (performance to quota, pipeline build, predictability on committed opportunities, adherence to the buying process). This will reduce ambiguity and make the weekly forecast call more proficient and factual as opposed to a storytelling exercise.

2 Develop your communication and check-in cadence. Consider a daily stand-up like the BMC huddle. This will create urgency in the forecast and a daily coaching opportunity.

3 Schedule a quarterly business review that looks back at the previous quarter's performance with the 4Ps and looks forward to the next two quarters with a close eye on commits and best-case opportunities.

6

Stone Four:
Performance

Tennis player Arthur Ashe said, "Success is a journey, not a destination. The doing is more important than the outcome." I have found that with the 5 Stones Growth Systems, the journey will lead you to the desired performance outcomes.

Health tech companies often obsess over performance while overlooking the fundamental building blocks that drive success. Sustainable performance is actually the natural outcome created through the journey of having tightly aligned systems in place.

The first three stones that we talked about—process, pipeline, and predictability—are all leading indicators that determine whether you're going to hit your performance and deliver ultimate shareholder value.

Obviously, with any investor, board, founder, or CEO I've ever worked for, performance to quota or hitting the bookings number is the single most important metric that drives revenue. And that is rightfully so. That's why we play the great game of business!

But it's interesting to see the number of companies that are unpredictable with their internal go-to-market strategies, yet they expect to be predictable with their performance. If you don't have the processes set up, if you don't have those first three stones in tight alignment sequentially, it's virtually impossible to be consistent with performance.

For this reason, performance could be the shortest chapter in this book. Once you get the machine running properly and are more predictable with your internal processes, growth and performance will accelerate. However, I think it's important to discuss a few outside factors that can impact performance.

Buy-In To Accelerate Growth And Reduce Drag

In their book, *What a Unicorn Knows: How Leading Entrepreneurs Use Lean Principles to Drive Sustainable Growth*, Matthew E. May and Pablo Dominguez lay out five lean scaleup principles, the first being strategic speed.[10]

To paraphrase, strategic speed in business is similar to what fighter pilots, professional cyclists, and race car drivers know that enables them to travel faster and farther with half the effort. They understand the importance of aerodynamics and the value of drafting in the slipstream created by those in front of you.

This also applies to increasing performance with your go-to-market team. It starts with buy-in to the process at the leadership level and an effective go-to-marketing strategy, where everyone is moving together toward a common goal with a clear understanding of their role and how they are expected to function and contribute to the overall organizational success.

In a startup or scaleup company, it must be a team game. If you have lone wolves who are not contributing to the organization's overall growth, you need to move on from them. There is no room for self-service or anyone with the personality to go rogue on the team to create division through gossip, petty politics, or a sense of entitlement.

I call it the diva wide receiver syndrome. In the NFL, in recent years, we have seen wide receivers who are very talented but are terrible for team chemistry. You can't keep them within the organization. It's the same for the go-to-market team culture. This unacceptable behavior will create dangerous drag on the organization, disrupting the strategic speed your team is working hard to create. And it will undoubtedly have a massive impact on the team's performance.

It doesn't matter if they have potential or are a steady performer. In the long run, it's best to move them out because they will create cancer for the team. I've had to do that. It's a tough decision to make. I sometimes use the example of one drop of poison in the punch ruining the party for everybody. That's exactly what happens when you have politics or a person with a bad attitude in your organization.

When Bookings Happen Related To Revenue Performance

Bookings are the tip of the spear to revenue. Working closely as a leadership team, it is imperative to understand how you set your forecasted booking and what the expectations of bookings are to billings as it relates to in-year revenue. Surprisingly, it's not uncommon to see startups do a peanut butter spread approach to setting quotas (evenly distributing them across the four quarters) and failing to apply historical trends such as summer seasonality, fiscal year trends, and year-end pushes.

This will all have a material impact on in-year revenue. Taking an annual quota and equally distributing it across all quarters is extremely problematic. Even with the best process and pipeline, not knowing these important trends will leave an organization playing catch-up or, worse yet, missing its annual numbers altogether.

Avoiding The Black Swan

Historically, all swans had been assumed to be white, so the term *black swan* was used to describe an impossible event. Imagine the surprise of the Dutch explorer Willem de Vlamingh when he found black swans in Australia in 1697. Just because something has not happened yet doesn't mean that it won't happen in the future. In other words, black swans are surprise events—but not all surprises are good.

Black swans involve a level deeper than understanding the customer. They require understanding specific situations unique to each individual health system. Black swans can appear in both net-new deals and with existing customers, and both can be major revenue kills if left undiscovered.

Here is an example of a black swan in the buying process. I was with an organization competing to win a large health system on the West Coast. Our key influencer learned that the department that would be using our software solution might be outsourced. If we had not had the right person and they had not been an advocate for our solution, we may have won the software selection battle, but lost the war once the leading outsourced company had been selected.

Because we had developed such a strong relationship and worked our process so well, we became a part of their team's decision process. We had done such an effective job of building trust and respect that the organization wanted to ensure we were a part of their way forward. They aligned us with the leading outsourcing candidate, and we built an integrated offering together. Without having the right key influencer, clearly defining the three whys, and leading them to make sense of the problem, we could have been blindsided and been the victim of a black swan.

An Example Of Performance In Action

This is the story of Brian, an eager AE who worked for me early in my career as a CRO. We had developed what we believed to be a strong commercial message, which, as we discussed earlier, is intended to get key influencers to think differently about their business and is a critical early-stage milestone in our buying process.

Through a referral, Brian secured a meeting for him and me with a large health system where we would try out our new messaging for the first time. This initial meeting included their team and the key influencer, which happened to be the health system CFO. The meeting started, and the CFO walked in a few minutes late, sat down, and started fiddling with his phone.

We're going through the presentation following the formula discussed earlier in the book, showing the client that we can connect with their pain at a deep level, which leads to a differentiated strategy that only our software can enable.

When we got to the strategy slide, or what I like to refer to as the money slide, we caught the CFO's attention.

The CFO laid his phone down, looked at the screen, and said, "I've never thought about it like that before." This changed the dynamic of the room and opened up the dialog, as we had developed credibility and respect with the group members. The call to action and takeaway from the meeting was that the CFO committed to bringing together the other department leads who would be affected by the decision.

Three weeks later, we completed a whiteboard session with the cross-departmental team, designed a compelling business case that was leveraged to advance the opportunity, and eventually won the deal.

Brian fully adopted the process, and his confidence level grew. I could count on Brian since he fully internalized the approach and followed it on every opportunity in his pipeline. Not to say his deals never slipped, but I could rely on him when he committed to a number and a deal, and I was rarely surprised. He became predictable and my top performer by adopting the process and leveraging it on all of his deals.

The goal is to build an entire team of Brians. You can't do that unless you have the right leading indicators or milestones that drive that lagging performance indicator.

Three Takeaways

1 As the company's leader, ensure the organization has bought into the go-to-market systems, particularly within the leadership team. The goal is to move together to create strategic speed. And don't wait until everything is perfect to start executing.

2 If there are people, processes, or politics holding you back, eliminate them immediately.

3 Be intentional about leveraging your buying process for increased visibility and alignment with your prospects to avoid black swans derailing your pipeline opportunities and growth.

7

Stone Five:
People

The *Sales Bible* author Jeffery Gitomer once said, "Most people will not do the hard work it takes to make success easy. Don't be like most people." I'll add to that: don't hire people who don't want it bad enough to put in the hard work, period.

It's critical that you hire the right people—the fifth stone—as they will drive the other four stones. To begin with, they need to be coachable. Looking back over my career, all of my top performers have embraced the system.

The people you hire need to be self-starters. They need to value toughness, be smart, and have grit. Working for a startup or scaleup company with limited resources and support is very different from working for a larger company. The people you hire need to think differently and have an entrepreneurial spirit.

I like to say I want salespeople who run angry. What I mean by that, as an NFL fan, is to watch how certain running backs hit the hole. The tough ones hit the hole with aggression, confidence, and trust in the play calling and the team surrounding them. That's the attitude required for the person who can step into a go-to-market role and follow the 5 Stones Growth Systems.

Your people need to also have a level of sophistication that goes beyond the stereotypical salesperson persona. Remember, you need someone who can operate within a predictable system so that they can be creative, unpredictable, and uncommon to separate themselves and you from all the noise in the market. They need to be bought into the fact that you are putting them in a position to win. When you place them on the battlefield, can they be a David?

Understanding The Three Types Of Sellers And Which Can Effectively Lead The 5 Stones Growth Systems

In my experience as a revenue leader, I have encountered three types of sellers. There is a clear winner among them when it comes to creating the purchase experience, as laid out in this book.

The "Salesman"

Think Alec Baldwin's character Blake from *Glenngary Glen Ross* discussed earlier in the book. This individual follows the traditional approach of discovery, demo, and propose. They are more concerned about selling the product than solving the prospect's problem. The dollar signs shine bright in their eyes for all to see, including the prospects. They don't have a clue how to lead a discussion to uncover hidden challenges for the client and feel extremely uncomfortable having a business conversation with a prospect.

They will never leave their comfort zone to push the status quo and never think of creating healthy tension, at least not for the right reasons. This individual will always revert back to price and give away margin at any cost. They can be aggressive and money-motivated, which can be misperceived as a good thing. Avoid this profile at all costs. If you have them in your existing sales team, save yourself some heartache and put them on a performance improvement plan.

The Content Curator, Aka The Information King

This type of seller is all about providing tons of information to try to hit the mark with a shotgun approach, hoping that something they provide will pique the prospect's interest. They utilize long, detailed PowerPoint presentations and bludgeon the prospect with a lengthy demo that covers everything from beginning to end, regardless of whether the prospect wants to hear it or not.

Like the salesman, they are not value-creation-oriented; for the most part, they are product-focused. When they follow up, their emails run paragraph after paragraph with multiple attachments with, you guessed it, more content.

Early in my career as a sales manager, an executive randomly called my cell phone upset and asked me to please have my rep stop sending him these lengthy emails with all the attachments. He said, "Please tell her I'm not reading them; she is wasting her time sending them." Needless to say, this profile is also a bad fit for the 5 Stones Growth Systems.

Both of these types of sellers are very predictable to the client and will do you more harm than good. They have self-limiting beliefs with their approach and rarely can be coached to get outside of their comfort zones to do something different and engaging for prospects. They are not capable of thinking differently and would probably fit better with a Goliath organization. That leads us to the ideal type of seller that matches the right profile to adopt the process outlined in this book.

The Facilitator

This person clearly understands the client's business and excels at problem-solving with decision-makers. They are capable of offering a customer a unique perspective about their business. They have strong communication skills and are confident and comfortable standing before a team of executives and leading a guided whiteboard discussion.

They need to know what moves the customer and be willing to dig to uncover unrecognized challenges around those things. They also need to be comfortable discussing ROI and finances and challenging customers to think differently about how to arrive at their desired outcomes.

They are confident in what their solution brings to the table and able to create healthy tension. Healthy tension is not challenging the customer from an aggressive perspective but having conviction in what their solution can do to affect the customer's business.

It's important to interview people with that frame of mind as you look for your talent and also to assess your current talent. At a minimum, you should be reassessing during quarterly business reviews. You must be willing to make decisions when things aren't working out. With smaller organizations, time is extremely important. You need people willing to follow the process that fits within the system. I like to use the EOS framework of GWC: get it, want it, and have the capacity to do it.[11]

Creating The Right Culture For Success

I often refer to culture as an intangible asset. It might lack physical form, but the value, knowledge, and innovation it drives are priceless.

The go-to-market team in a startup or scaleup must be in complete alignment. Everyone must be clear on the organization's why, completely bought into the strategy to execute, and aligned on what's important to grow the company. As we mentioned earlier, there is no room for entitlement. Yes, we all get into sales to make money, but there needs to be a higher understanding that helping a company grow can open up a lifetime of opportunities. For less tenured members of the go-to-market team, this might be more difficult to grasp.

One of the key conversations I always have during the hiring process and constantly preach to the team is that being a part of a successful startup or scaleup will serve them for the rest of their careers. For most sellers, their current stop with your organization will most likely not be their last. In fact, studies have shown that the average tenure for a SaaS salesperson is 2.5 years.

Based on this understanding, I share with them that they will learn a process and be a part of something that most other candidates they compete against in the future will simply not understand. They will be on the company's front line of revenue growth and will be able to specifically share how they helped a company scale as an individual contributor with conviction.

Not only that, but by being a part of a smaller company, they will have access to experience how other departments function and see exactly how their contribution affects all other areas within the organization. They will get a crash course in entrepreneurship, which is as valuable for career growth as the commission check they'll receive for making it happen. It's really important that you hire and retain people who get that. We are all selfish by nature, but understanding and aligning with this concept will ensure buy-in and promote a growth mentality with the entire team.

I mentioned in chapter 2 that one of the ten growth killers I have seen is losing accountability for OKRs and other key initiatives that are critical to growth. Creating a culture of inclusion that highlights everyone's value in the company's success and an entrepreneurial mindset with each team member will lead to ownership of your key strategic initiatives.

An Environment For Open Expression

For the go-to-market team, and honestly, for the company as a whole, you need to create an environment of psychological safety. Paul Santagata, when head of industry at Google, said, "There is no team without trust."[12] And so, it's extremely important that the leadership team and everyone in the organization trust each other, which promotes a feeling of safety.

To create psychological safety, you need to ensure that everybody in the organization knows it's okay to make mistakes without fear of punishment. It's okay to take moderate risks, and you should encourage that.

The feeling of safety promotes creativity. I often refer to the buying process strategy as guardrails. The guardrails actually create a zone where creativity can grow because boundaries are clear. Mistakes are more easily identified and corrected within the system, providing a controlled environment for moderate risk-taking. This allows individuals to be themselves and creative in the process, and it opens you up as a leader to feel comfortable encouraging that.

As you'll learn through forecast reviews, there are going to be certain milestones within the process that are nonnegotiable. But at the end of the day, we need to encourage creativity. We don't want robots out there because we want to foster relationships and respect with the organizations that we're calling on.

Everybody needs to feel free to speak their mind. I always tell my teams, "It's okay to tell me that you disagree with me. I promise I won't shut you down as long as you do it respectfully. I'll listen to what you have to say. Then, we're going to make a decision together on how we will proceed.

We're not going to look back once we make that decision, and I'm wide open to hearing a better way. Because the bottom line is that we're constantly looking to find better ways to grow the business. Everyone needs to feel like they can stick their neck out without getting it cut off."

When you do all that, it eliminates the feeling of panic and being attacked. People become more curious and more confident. They're easier to inspire. Your meetings will become more social. Everyone will be more open-minded to things because they know they won't get belittled for expressing a different opinion. People will be more resilient because they believe you have their back as an organization. They'll be more motivated and more persistent.

They will feel safe. I've found that when your organization matures in the area of psychological safety, your employees will trust you more and actually challenge each other!

Creating A Safe Environment In Action

I want to share a conversation that brings the above to life. I went to an organization, and we were about to have our first quarterly business review.

Just before the meeting I received a text from one of my previous AEs who I mentioned earlier in the book, Brian. I told him I would love to catch up with him, but I was getting ready to start my first QBR with a new team, and we were preparing to go live. His response to me was, "Can I sit in and challenge people? LOL."

That's when you have psychological safety. It's not the leader questioning certain things about performance or ideas; it's the actual peers doing it. That's when the magic starts happening. When there is buy-in across the organization, people are actively engaged in growth and having fun. This is a team game, not an individual game. This is about growing the company. It's understanding that if I help another AE win a large deal, it will also benefit me.

This is where you can help your team eliminate any sense of entitlement and work for the better of the group. As mentioned earlier, there is no room for divas here. This goes beyond humility to humanity. The team understands their purpose, and works together to that purpose: to get the win and defeat the Goliath competitor.

The numbers also support this endeavor. According to studies conducted by Gartner, Gallup, and *Harvard Business Review*, employees who feel psychologically safe in their organization and role have significantly better performance, including 50 percent higher productivity, 76 percent more engagement, and 27 percent less turnover.[13] This has a massive and often overlooked impact on revenue at the end of the day.

Hiring Your Revenue Leader

When it comes time to hire a revenue leader, think about David. He was someone who was fearless, comfortable in his own skin, and had a history of success. Your revenue leader must have a player-coach mentality. This person must be willing to roll up their sleeves and get their hands dirty.

I've often seen situations where organizations hire somebody with a big contact list. Eventually, the contact list runs dry, and you are simply left with someone who knows a lot of people but can't help you grow.

Please don't misunderstand me. I am not saying that having a robust contact list is a bad thing. But if it is the only thing your future revenue leader is bringing to the equation, you won't get very far. They have to have a process mindset and a boots-on-the-ground mentality.

Then I see organizations think, I'll hire a big GE, IBM-type revenue leader. It's not about the title but about being a true operating executive. Rarely do those people understand how to operate within a startup or scaleup environment by rolling up their sleeves and getting dirty. They will often try to distance themselves from the frontlines by hiring unneeded layers that just add to CAC (Customer Acquisition Cost) without delivering results. Instead, look for someone who has worked for smaller companies with a track record of building out teams and processes from the ground up. Someone who is a true leader and leads from the front. Someone who understands how to teach by example to gain credibility with the internal team and external prospects.

You also need somebody who is willing to challenge you as a CEO because sometimes you need to hear it. They cannot crumble under certain pressures. They need to be willing to step up and have difficult conversations. They need to be someone who understands how to leverage data to support their position and support you in front of a board in a credible and believable way.

I highly recommend that you have your revenue leader candidates present their process to the executive leadership team in a group setting. This gives you the ability to not only test out their process but also allows you to see how they present and how they might handle themselves with prospects when they need to think on their feet. This includes how they are with executive presence. It's uncomfortable, but it can provide valuable information before you make the offer. In fact, I would recommend the same process when hiring AEs for the same reason. The cost associated with making a mistake in a smaller health tech company versus a billion-dollar one is extremely different and has a massive impact on the business, especially at the leadership level, but is equally important at the AE level as well.

A cost-effective option can be to bring on a fractional revenue leader to set up and kickstart your go-to-market systems at a much more rapid pace. A fractional revenue leader is someone with experience and a track record of success who works for the organization on a part-time or project basis, providing leadership expertise. They are a 1099 employee which eliminates cost for things such as benefits and equity. They can also be a great addition to the leadership team as they bring an outside perspective. When the time is right, they can help you coach up an internal candidate to move into the leadership role or provide the go-to-market leadership recruitment expertise to bring on the right revenue leader.

Your process, pipeline, predictability, and performance must be in place to slot in the final piece of the puzzle: your people. People and the culture they create can solidify your puzzle into a powerhouse or derail all of your work in a single stroke. I have developed the 5 Stones Growth Systems through many battles with Goliaths over my career. When you are intentional about its execution, you will take down your giants and drive predictable and repeated growth.

The questions then become: How do you sustain use of the 5 Stones Growth Systems, how are you showing that they make dollars and sense, and what comes next?

Three Takeaways

1 Develop hiring profiles and optimal personas for what you are looking for with your go-to-market team. Evaluate your current team for fit to ensure they GWC: get it, want it, and are capable of doing it.

2 Evaluate your culture to determine if you are creating the right environment to attract and retain right-fit AEs who can thrive within a startup or scaleup. Determine if you have a psychologically safe environment that promotes moderate risk-taking and creativity.

3 Define what you are looking for in a revenue leader. Do you have it today? How do you find it if you don't, and could a fractional revenue leader be an option?

PART III

What Comes Next

As we examined in prior chapters, the 5 Stones Growth Systems can set up your organization to allow your people to perform with predictability internally, leveraging a framework for success when executed in the right sequence, with the right mindset and buy-in across the organization. This, in turn, will create an uncommon approach to your go-to-market execution that changes the dynamic of the battlefield when competing against better-funded health tech Goliaths. This is, in essence, looking back at the systems you have in place to optimize them to position your company for a competitive edge to outmaneuver and win more consistently.

Now, we cast ourselves forward and discuss how to measure the go-to-market team's success for scale. We will look forward, but we will also look back at how COVID-19 took some things away from us that, quite frankly, we need to return to again. In addition, we'll look at the evolving landscape with components such as AI and where your focus should be to stay on track over the coming years.

I will also answer the question of whether the 5 Stones Growth Systems will only work in health tech, which I am often asked. Finally, I will close with a call to action to break through the anxiety of your leadership position and unlock the potential of your organization and team, setting you up as a modern-day warrior, ready to face your giants.

8

The Math Behind
The Solutions

Neil deGrasse Tyson famously said, "Math is the language of the universe."[14] It should also be the language of your health tech organization. It removes vagueness and keeps your company on track.

Tightly managing the 5 Stones Growth Systems will provide you with the data you need to address the financial equation of growth as to when and how to invest in the go-to-market team. Often, the decision to add AEs or SDRs or invest in marketing is based on feel and not math.

As a reminder, the 5 Stones Growth Systems metrics are process, pipeline, predictability, and performance, referred to earlier as the 4Ps dashboard. Those are key ingredients for your forecasting capabilities, assessing talent, and daily business management to understand if you have healthy sales territories.

There are three other metrics that I would add to track in addition to the 4Ps. The first is annual contract value (ACV), to see if it is trending up or down. Tracking this metric will tell you a lot, from margins on deals to how you are executing your enterprise strategy.

The second metric to add is deal velocity. By leading the purchase experience, you should see opportunities accelerate; if not, it provides the leading indicator to explore where the delays might occur.

Finally, track conversion rates on all of your go-to-market activities. We discussed the marketing formulas earlier in the pipeline chapter, but you should also track conversion rates for all pipeline activities whether it be for your channel program, SDR team, or AE self-generated pipeline. This will tell you what to continue doing, what to stop doing, and where you need to start investing more.

I already mentioned key metrics of logo retention and churn, as well as gross and net revenue retention, as critical metrics for managing and creating growth with your existing client base, so we will skip past those as well in this section. However, these metrics are critical to any leadership scorecard.

The next phase includes the metrics to manage the health and scalability of the go-to-market business itself. I have always developed strong relationships with my CFOs, as designing these reports and managing them should be a collaborative effort and a part of the executive team's scorecard.

There can be a host of metrics to track for a deep dive into the business, but I have found that the following key data points can paint a quick picture of the go-to-market team's performance. They will drive the discussion on gaps and growth and provide the unit economics to make critical decisions.

Customer Acquisition Cost (CAC)

CAC is the cost to acquire one new customer. It can be calculated in several different ways. You can base it on pass-through costs alone, such as marketing spend and software, or you can include the cost of people who are involved as well (AEs, SDRs, marketing, etc.).

If you choose to go at it from the more detailed route, which I recommend, you will need to determine the cost of your go-to-market team. Marketing and SDRs are pretty straightforward for the most part as they are usually salary plus bonus, but the sales team can be a whole different story.

I've seen a wide range of salaries and variable comp packages within the same sales organization. I will discuss AE compensation later in this chapter as it can have a material impact on CAC.

The formula to determine CAC is sales and marketing expenses divided by the number of customers acquired over a given time period. The CAC ratio measures new and expansion annual recurring revenue (ARR). It is calculated by taking sales and marketing expenses and dividing them by the total new and expansion dollars of ARR over a given time period.

$$CAC = \frac{\text{Sales \& Marketing Expenses}}{\text{Number Of Customers Acquired}}$$

CAC Payback

This calculates the number of months it takes an organization to recoup its investment in sales and marketing. It is best to calculate this metric by looking at gross margin, as that is the most accurate way to determine how long it takes to recoup the actual cost.

The formula for calculating CAC payback is sales and marketing expenses divided by net new MRR (monthly reoccurring revenue) times gross margin percent.

Leveraging your CAC and the payback period can help your organization make informed decisions on when and how to increase spend. Examples could be implementing and scaling channels like trade shows, ICP engagement events, expanding engagements with media outlets, and adding paid marketing as discussed in chapter 4.

$$\frac{\text{CAC}}{\text{Payback}} = \frac{\text{Sales \& Marketing Expense}}{\text{Net New MRR x Gross Margin \%}}$$

Average Revenue Per Account (ARPA)

As it sounds, this measures the average revenue generated from each customer over a given time period. The formula for calculating ARPA is to take the revenue during a given time period and divide it by the number of accounts your organization has during the same time period.

$$\text{ARPA} = \frac{\text{Revenue Over "X" Time Period}}{\text{Number Of Accounts During Same Time Period}}$$

Lifetime Value (LTV)

This is the total amount of revenue a company can expect to generate from a single customer throughout their entire lifetime with your company. It basically tells you how much a customer is worth over the entire time they are a client. The formula to calculate LTV is to take ARPA and divide it by your churn rate.

$$\text{LTV} = \frac{\text{Average Revenue Per Account}}{\text{Revenue Churn}}$$

CAC To LTV Ratio (CAC:LTV)

This is the total revenue you can expect during the lifetime of the average customer for every dollar you spend to acquire that customer. This ratio is an important metric as it quickly tells you how your go-to-market spend is affecting the overall health of your company's revenue.

For example, if your ratio is 1:1, it means that for every dollar you spend, you are making one dollar. For a startup, this might not be as alarming as it would be for a more mature organization. However, it's something that needs to be monitored monthly as you want to see the ratio improve or changes will need to be made.

As a rule of thumb, a 1:3 ratio is considered healthy and anything approaching 1:5 or greater indicates that, for a company that is looking to scale fast, more investments should be made in the go-to-market function. The formula to calculate CAC:LTV is LTV divided by CAC.

$$\text{LTV:CAC} = \frac{\text{LTV}\left(\dfrac{\text{Average Revenue Per Customer}}{\text{Revenue Churn}}\right)}{\text{CAC}\left(\dfrac{\text{Sales \& Marketing Expense}}{\text{Number Of Customers Acquired}}\right)}$$

The Compensation Question

As mentioned above, compensation can affect your metrics, especially when looking at CAC, CAC payback, and CAC:LTV. I want to focus on AE compensation, as it typically creates the greatest variable. Still, I will also discuss how I typically compensate other members of the go-to-market team.

AEs

The AE compensation plan holds the greatest variable and impact on the metrics discussed in this chapter. The typical compensation structure for AEs is a base salary and a variable compensation plan. To set the variable component to align with the overall compensation, I set a quota of five times their total compensation package.

For example, if your AE has a $200,000 compensation package, the quota should be $1 million to achieve on-target earnings. You also should see a new AE tracking toward their quota within six months of being hired.

If you offer a signing bonus or guarantee, I like to tie the payout to leading indicators of success. Examples are completing a territory plan, completing x number of discovery calls or commercial messaging discussions and other key milestones, building x amount of pipeline, time to first closed/won opportunity, etc.

Head Of Marketing

We have all heard the saying that compensation drives performance and behaviors. For this reason, in addition to base salary, I like to include a bucket of variable comp dollars that I can tie to quarterly OKRs such as pipeline, conversion rates, and quarterly bookings from marketing activities. I also like to create an annual bonus tied to bookings, which ensures integration between the sales and marketing teams.

SDRs

Typically, I provide a base salary and a variable compensation per meeting booked/held. I also like to add in another variable compensation component for pipeline generation. This helps to incentivize the SDRs to go after larger prospects rather than play it safe with smaller ones. It takes as much energy and resources to pursue a large client as it does a small one. Encourage your SDRs to think bigger.

RevOps And Sales Enablement

If you have the budget for these positions, I like to include a base salary and, much like marketing, provide a bucket of comp dollars for quarterly OKRs and an annual bookings bonus. As I will discuss in the next chapter, these roles will become more prevalent in smaller companies as AI continues to become more embedded in sales and marketing.

Start Tracking Now

If you are not tracking these metrics now, I highly recommend adding them to your existing scorecard. It's important to create a baseline and then start measuring how they are trending as you add headcount, implement marketing initiatives and strategies, and invest in new tools.

Having this information will ensure the monthly board meetings are focused on strategy and execution. If you are looking to add investors, these will be critical metrics to paint a picture of your go-to-market strategy's success and give a clear view of how investments will be used to grow market share.

In addition, these metrics will help with the annual planning process and justify any pivots or adjustments that need to occur throughout the year. At the end of the day, it will help apply science to decisions that are typically random, reactive, and treated as a guessing game.

Now that you have understood and are applying the 5 Stone Growth Systems with math to support strategic decisions, what's next? And what future trends can be leveraged to amplify your growth?

Three Takeaways

1 Create a scorecard to start tracking the key metrics mentioned in the chapter to determine the health of your go-to-market strategy. Begin using these numbers to drive healthy conversations with the leadership team, board, and investors.

2 Determine which programs are contributing to growth and which ones are not in order to uncover opportunities to increase investments or take corrective action.

3 Evaluate compensation programs for all your go-to-market team members to ensure that their on-target earnings package drives the right behaviors and is within range of a healthy CAC.

9

Back To The Future

When envisioning the future of health tech and go-to-market strategies, I'm reminded of Marty McFly's journey in *Back to the Future*. Ironically, our path forward requires reclaiming valuable practices we left behind during the COVID-19 pandemic.

The most significant casualty I've observed in organizations post-COVID is genuine human connection. My experience consistently shows that on-site engagement and face-to-face value creation dramatically improve client decision-making processes.

Whiteboard sessions and in-person interactions allow us to read subtle emotional cues, maintain focus without digital distractions, and facilitate authentic conversations impossible to replicate through screens. This isn't merely anecdotal—as detailed in chapter 3, when buying committees commit to in-person whiteboard sessions, my teams have achieved an extraordinary 90 percent win rate.

We've lost the art of personal engagement, and rekindling it is crucial. Being physically present helps clients make sense of complex problems through real-time collaboration and dynamic thinking.

While this approach isn't necessary for every transaction, it's invaluable for significant deals involving multiple decision-makers—which describes most enterprise healthcare sales. Remember our central premise: in this industry, groups make decisions, not individuals. Face-to-face interaction builds the relationships and earns the respect essential for navigating complex buying committees.

Looking To The Future To Enhance Human Engagement

I recently worked with a behavioral health software company where the importance of human engagement has never been more obvious. When individuals are suffering from substance use disorder, group therapy and constant support through human-to-human interaction is critical to someone's recovery.

The recovery becomes a journey that is grounded in meeting with others for support for the rest of an individual's life. Providers in the field realize that they must engage personally to gain a deep understanding of the trauma behind the pain, develop relationships, and establish trust.

For this reason, AI in behavioral health is focused on reducing administrative tasks so that more time can be spent with the patient. When looking at go-to-market trends for the next three years with AI and other tools, I see a parallel path. Creating the opportunity to improve efficiencies for better human-to-human engagement will be critical to creating predictable growth, especially for the startup and scaleup communities.

Effective Tools To Help With Remote Engagement

Creating in-person human engagement is important; however, it is not always possible or cost-effective. As a result, we need to find ways to engage better through virtual meetings.

I have mentioned the skill of using a whiteboard throughout the book. It is one of the single most effective collaboration and consensus-building skills anyone can master. However, it's nearly impossible to do it remotely without the right technology. To teach the process virtually, I recently added the Vibe Board to my training tools. It is a fifty-five-inch virtual whiteboard that allows for remote collaboration through any video conferencing app. The product has been game-changing for me and a great example of how to use technology to improve human-to-human interaction remotely.

Artificial Intelligence Impact

Obviously, the hot topic right now is AI, and there are a lot of tools that can help with process documentation in the CRM, creating efficiencies in communications from SDR and AE outreach, and content creation. There is also sophisticated conversational intelligence to analyze recorded engagement with prospects to ensure key milestones were discussed.

As we all know, the AI market is exploding. In fact, some projections[15] have an expected compound annual growth rate of 27.67 percent from 2025 to 2030, reaching a market volume of $826.73 billion by 2030.

If you haven't developed a strategy for AI with your go-to-market teams, you are already behind. Considering the speed of development, I am not going to focus on the technology but rather on what you need to do to prepare for the seismic shift we are experiencing.

It is important to understand that AI, as it exists today for go-to-market, is really machine learning. I recently attended a presentation at my alma mater by John Connaughton, Director of Economic Forecasting with the Belk College of Business at the University of North Carolina Charlotte, where he said, "AI still doesn't replace gray matter, at least not yet."[16]

So the question becomes, how do you support your company's gray matter (in this case, your company's go-to-market team) by supporting AI tools as they rapidly evolve to keep up with the growth curve? The goal, as we discussed earlier, should be leveraging AI to improve efficiencies with your go-to-market team to automate manual, time-consuming tasks for enhanced personal engagement.

AI Data Management

We have all heard the term *garbage in, garbage out*. Take that expression and place it on steroids when discussing the future of AI and revenue growth. Data doesn't lie, but it does when it's garbage, incomplete at painting a picture or telling a story, or simply nonexistent. Poor adherence to and documentation of a buying process will absolutely derail any AI strategy to improve forecasting and predictability in your go-to-market execution.

To put it another way, if you haven't designed your buying process as discussed in this book, where milestones are tracked in a repeatable way that creates a standard shorthand language and generates standardized data points in your CRM, you need to start now.

One of the greatest challenges has always been to integrate sales and marketing. The access to external data through AI for the marketing team on competition, SEO, and intent, coupled with internally generated data from the buying process, will force the integration to drive an effective AI strategy.

Increased Focus On RevOps

I have found that one of the last hires with most startups and scaleups has often been with RevOps. Usually, a marketing lead or someone on the sales team will assume the role of the CRM admin. There is only so much budget to go around, so I understand this practice.

However, with data management now becoming ten times more of a priority in the age of AI, having a dedicated individual(s) to ensure data integrity in the CRM will become a top priority. In addition, the tech stack will become more complex and require more expertise rather than simply being another hat for a novice team member to wear.

Training Using AI

Training is one of the most challenging activities for a startup or scaleup. Like RevOps, it is typically not a priority, and SMEs within the organization are tasked with wearing yet another hat to make it happen.

AI should have a profound impact on training. It will make creating content for a learning management system easier, more effective in assessing skill gaps, and more efficient in automating role plays for real-time feedback, to name a few benefits. In addition, many aspects of sales enablement will be automated for tasks such as competitive analysis, updating and creating presentations, populating RFPs, and real-time coaching.

Enterprise Health Tech To Follow Social Selling

We have discussed the social nature of leveraging key influencers within organizations, much like those in social media. This will continue outside of the facility's four walls and spill into platforms we use in our everyday lives.

Much of our society today is addicted to scrolling, and as a result, screen times have increased significantly over the past ten years.[17] Leveraging content from influencers will be a growing strategy for marketing teams. In fact, we discussed a version of the concept in chapter 4 when we discussed our trade show strategy of interviewing thought leaders and pushing the content out on LinkedIn and other social media platforms.

Pricing models such as entry level tiered pricing or freemiums will become more prevalent in driving adoption, especially for startups and scaleups. To clarify, freemium is the strategy of offering a basic version of a product for free while charging for additional features and services. We see it all the time with apps for our phones. We are beginning to see it with enterprise solutions such as sales enablement tools and CRMs. It will be a common practice for health tech over the coming years.

10

Adaptability Of
The Systems

N ecessity is the mother of invention, but adaptability is the favorite aunt. In terms of adaptability, the smartest CEOs will take systems and make them their own.

If you have read this far, I assume you are a leader for an enterprise health tech company. However, I am often asked by leaders in other verticals if the 5 Stones Growth Systems only applies to healthcare. I would hope that based on the principles discussed in this book, it is clear that the 5 Stones Growth Systems can apply to any business:

- Understanding your why and what makes your organization unique should be a question that any CEO in any vertical and anyone on their team should be able to answer on autopilot.

- Confirming that you have a deep understanding of your target market and ensuring that you focus on the organizations your solution can affect the fastest should be a common understanding.
- Having a system for how you will execute to make you different with a buying process geared to create a unique experience for your prospect regardless of market should be a priority for predictable growth.
- Developing cost-effective, high-touch pipeline strategies in an omnichannel approach should be the lifeblood of any company, especially those in startup and scaleup mode.
- Leveraging your why, who you target, how you execute, and being intentional about building pipeline should lead to believable forecasting and predictability metrics with anyone.
- Hiring the right people who can lead compelling value-creation discussions and challenge current thinking should not be specific to just healthcare.
- And finally, driving the lagging indicator of performance with proven, predictable systems should be the goal of every CEO to create consistent performance and shareholder value.

In short, the 5 Stones Growth Systems is not specific to healthcare. It is a system that can transform any organization, including health tech.

11

No One Is Coming
To Save You

avid went to battle the giant alone. I always find this story fascinating in that both the Philistines and the nation of Israel were putting the fate of both of their nations in the hands of two warriors. I believe it's really not that much different than modern times when you, as the CEO of a startup or scaleup, are going to battle against the CEO of larger organizations or the Goliaths of your industry. Sure, you might have more people supporting you and handling the day-to-day and frontline execution, but the plan is all on you. You can have the support of the board and the investors, but you were put in your position to own the battle.

I'm sure that David felt the pressure and the feeling of isolation, but he had confidence in his purpose and process. Like you, he knew that he only had one shot at best, and I know that sandwich of emotions that you are feeling because I've been there. On one side, you have the incredible responsibility of the well-being of your team and their families; on the other, you have the pressure to deliver on the numbers coming from the top every month.

I'll never forget a comment that one of my mentors told me early in my career: "Get it right because no one is coming to save you." How confident are you in your current go-to-market strategy? Do you have the confidence and faith of David that your current path will create consistent and scalable growth for your company? Because your success or failure is up to you. No one is coming to save you. If you can't say yes to these two questions with confidence, then I highly recommend implementing the 5 Stones Growth Systems to create predictable growth as it has for other leaders just like you.

Appendix

Acknowledgments

I would like to start by thanking God for all of the opportunities and experiences that he has blessed me with during my life. Without him by my side guiding my steps, the wins and rebounds from the losses in life would never have been possible.

Second, I would like to thank my dad, Fred Sr. His toughness in the face of adversity and his love for his family made him the most honorable man that I have ever known. We deeply miss him, and I would like to dedicate this book to his memory.

Next, I would like to thank my mom, Ina, for always putting her family first. She's a tough lady with a sweet soul who has always been a steady rock for us all.

I would also like to thank all the companies and leaders who have provided me with the opportunities and experiences to develop the 5 Stones Growth Systems.

Additionally, I would like to call out a few individual contributors to the systems and processes discussed in this book. Shout out to Dan Furhmann, Steve Ganjoo, Kim Story, Cole Field, Colt Briner, and all of the amazing AEs, marketers, SDRs, and managers who I have worked with over the years. Y'all are awesome!

Finally, I would like to thank my beautiful wife, Victoria. She's *always* there supporting me, encouraging me, pushing me, and, most importantly, unconditionally loving me. This has been a dream come true for me, and it would not have been possible without her unwavering belief in me.

About The Author

Fred Sheffield has a twenty-five-year history of transforming sales and marketing organizations into multimillion-dollar revenue producers, introducing structure, discipline, and process rigor critical in leading teams to win against much larger, well-funded competitors.

As a chief revenue officer for multiple health tech SaaS companies and former general manager at organizations ranging from startups to market leaders, Fred specializes in building systems that deliver scalable and predictable growth. He is known for overhauling go-to-market strategies, reconfiguring sales and marketing organizations for optimal performance, and introducing formal sales processes, structure, and KPIs where none existed. As a result, companies that work with Fred to lead their go-to-market strategies have consistently seen high double-digit annual revenue growth, numerous five-times pipelines, and bookings growth of up to 66 percent year-over-year.

Over his years of experience, Fred has created the method called the 5 Stones Growth Systems, focused on helping startups and scaleups compete more effectively by being more predictable internally, less predictable externally, and winning the value-creation game.

Fred lives in Charlotte, North Carolina, with his wife, Victoria, and two Maltese pups, Axl and Mazzy. When he's not with his family (daughter Francesca, son-in-law Ty, and grandsons Ryder and Doss) attending Carolina Panthers football games, you will find Fred searching for that little white ball on the golf course.

Fred is ready to work with your organization, health tech or otherwise. Be sure to visit www.5stonesgrowth.com to find additional resources and reach out to Fred to chat more about how he can help your organization win against larger competitors: fred@5stonesgrowth.com.

Works Cited

1   1 Sam. 17:31–40, 17:49–51 (New King James Version).

2   Malcolm Gladwell, *David and Goliath: Underdogs, Misfits, and the Art of Battling Giants* (Back Bay Books, 2015).

3   *The Top 12 Reasons Startups Fai*l, CB Insights, 2021, https://www. cbinsights.com/reports/CB-Insights_Top-Reasons-Startups-Fail. pdf.

4   "Fast Facts US Health System," AHA Annual Survey Database FY2021, accessed March 12, 2025, https://www.aha.org/ system/files/media/file/2023/04/Fast-Facts-US-Health-Systems-Infographic-2023.pdf.

5   "Updated Report: Hospital and Corporate Acquisition of Physician Practices and Physician Employment 2019-2023," Physician's Advisory Institute, accessed March added12, 2025, https://www.physiciansadvocacyinstitute.org/Portals/0/ assets/docs/PAI-Research/PAI-Avalere%20Physician%20 Employment%20Trends%20Study%202019-2023%20Final. pdf?ver=uGHF46u1GSeZgYXMKFyYvw%3D%3D.

6   Matthew Dixon and Brent Adamson, *The Challenger Sale: Taking Control of the Customer Conversation*, (Portfolio, 2011).

7   Jeff Thull, *The Prime Solution: Close the Value Gap, Increase Margins, and Win the Complex Sale* (Kaplan, 2005).

8   *State of Sales*, 6th ed. (Salesforce, 2024), p. 12, https://www.salesforce.com/content/dam/web/en_us/www/documents/research/salesforce-state-of-sales-report-6-ed.pdf.

9   Chet Holmes, *The Ultimate Sales Machine: Turbocharge Your Business with Relentless Focus on 12 Key Strategies* (Portfolio, 2008).

10 Matthew E. May and Pablo Dominguez, *What a Unicorn Knows: How Leading Entrepreneurs Use Lean Principles to Drive Sustainable Growth* (Matt Holt, 2023).

11 Mark O'Donnell, "GWC™—The Difference Between 'Capacity' and 'Get It,'" EOS Mastery (blog), EOS, accessed February 26, 2025, https://www.eosworldwide.com/blog/difference-between-capacity-and-get-it.

12 Laura Delizonna, "High-Performing Teams Need Psychological Safety: Here's How to Create It," *Harvard Business Review*, August 24, 2017, https://hbr.org/2017/08/high-performing-teams-need-psychological-safety-heres-how-to-create-it.

13 Jon Minnick, "How Psychological Safety Affects Employee Productivity," Workplace Wellness, Ragan, April 14, 2023, https://www.ragan.com/how-psychological-safety-affects-employee-productivity/.

14 Neil deGrasse Tyson (@neiltyson), "Math is the language of the universe," Twitter, November 21, 2011, https://x.com/neiltyson/status/138764638438424577.

15 "Artificial Intelligence—Worldwide," Statista, accessed February 26, 2025, https://www.statista.com/outlook/tmo/artificial-intelligence/worldwide.

16   John Connaughton, Director of Economic Forecasting, (presentation), Belk College of Business, University of North Carolina, Charlotte, North Carolina.

17   Fabio Duarte, "Alarming Average Screen Time Statistics (2024)," Exploding Topics (blog), February 21, 2025, https://explodingtopics.com/blog/screen-time-stats.

Index